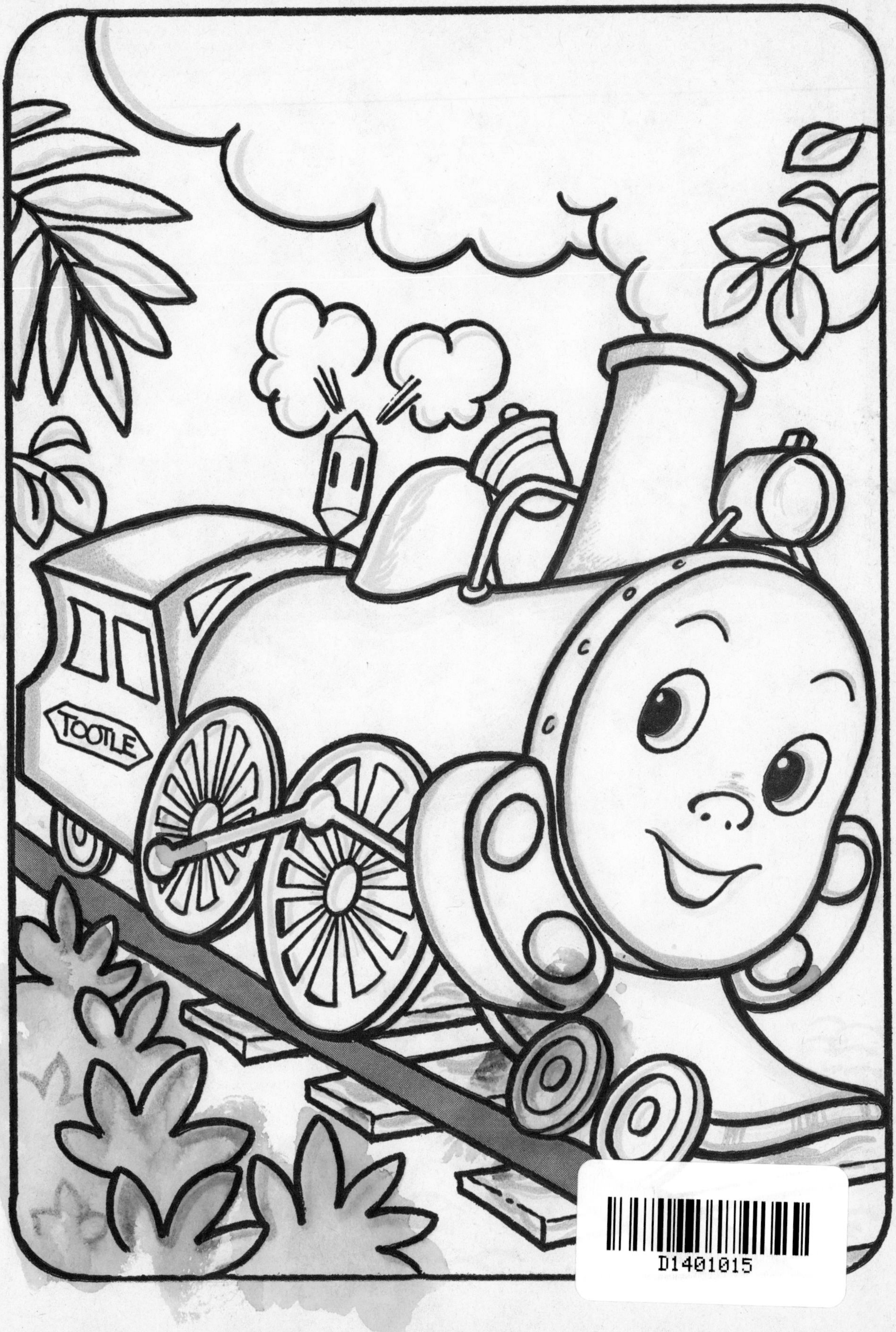
TOOTLE

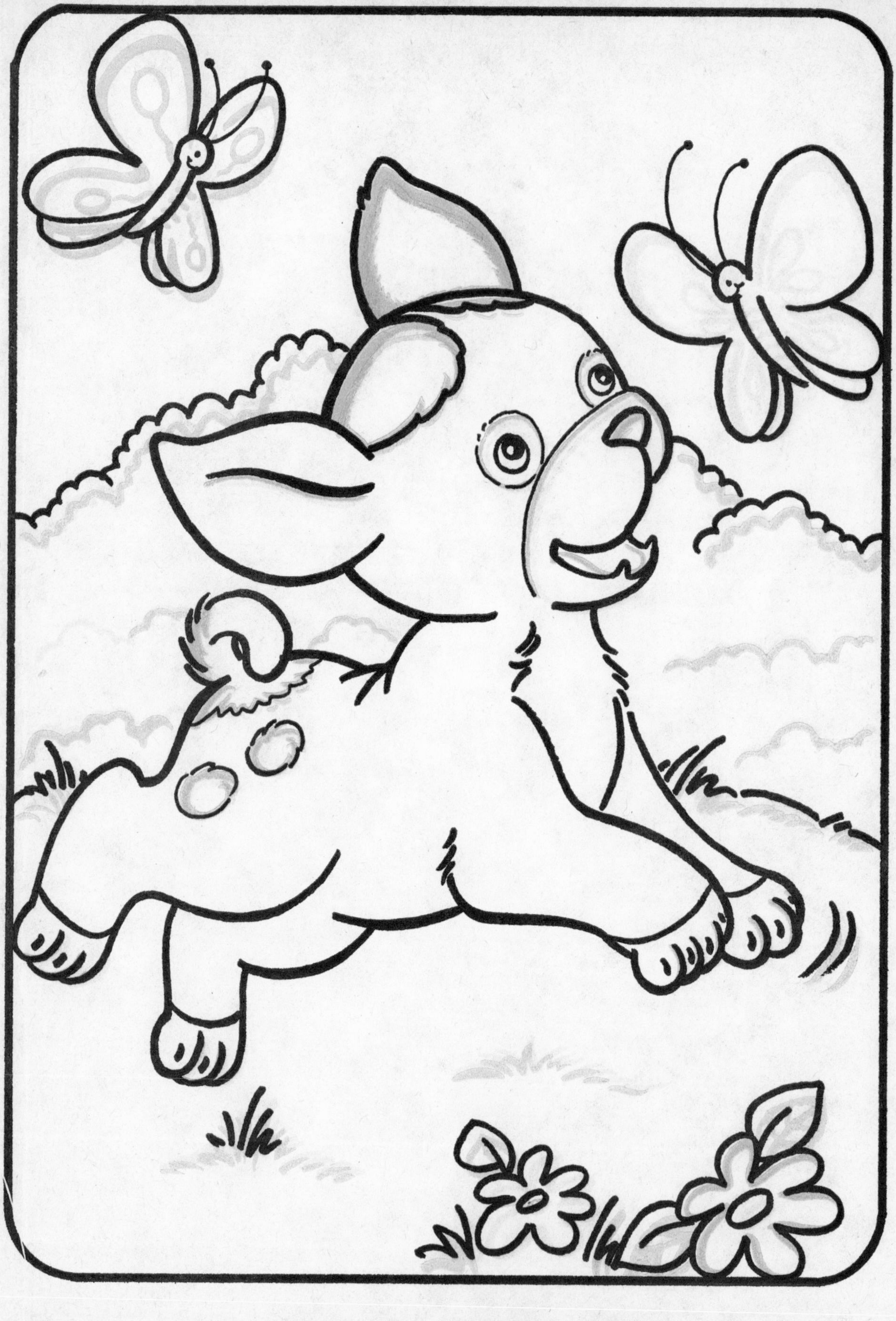

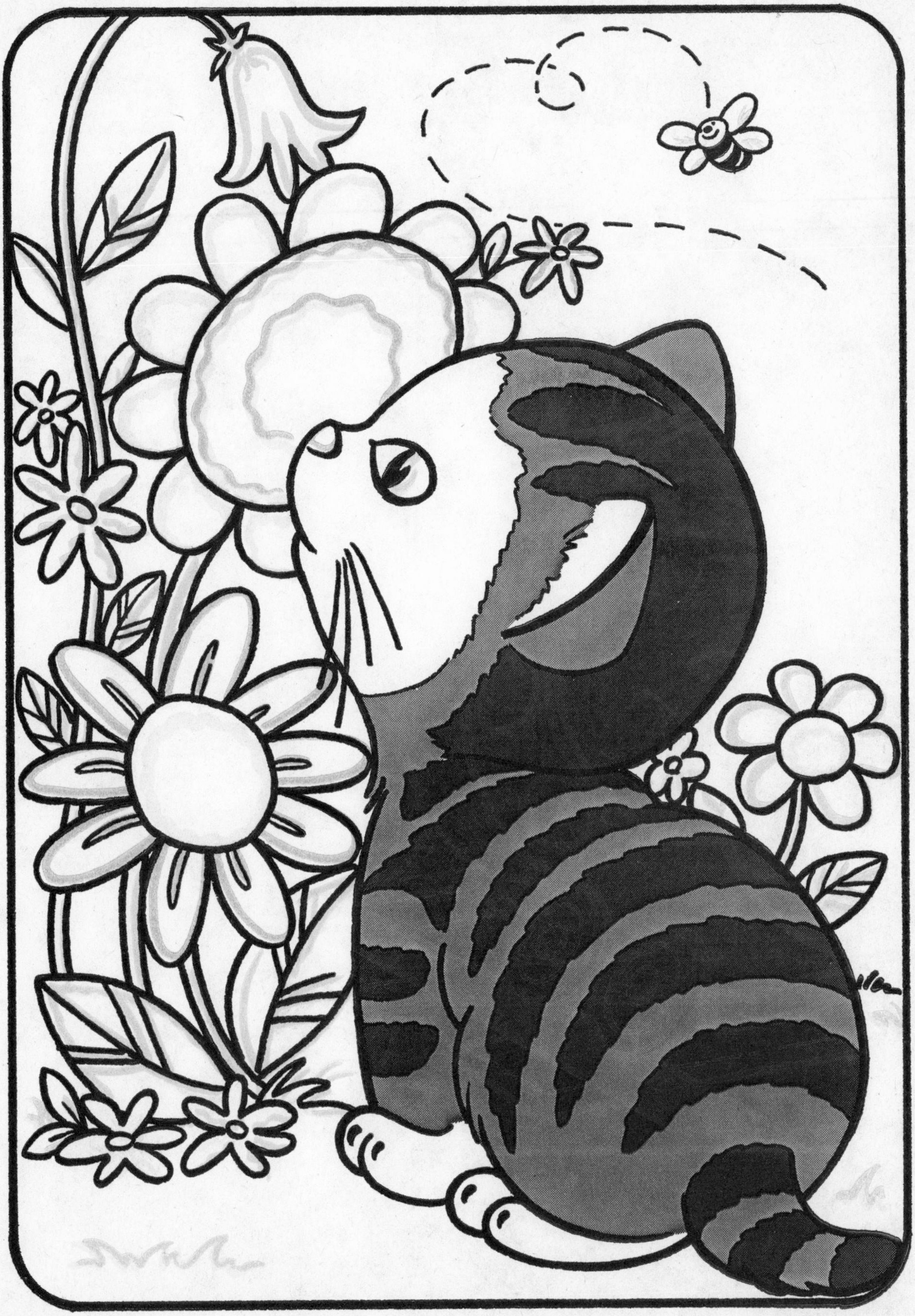

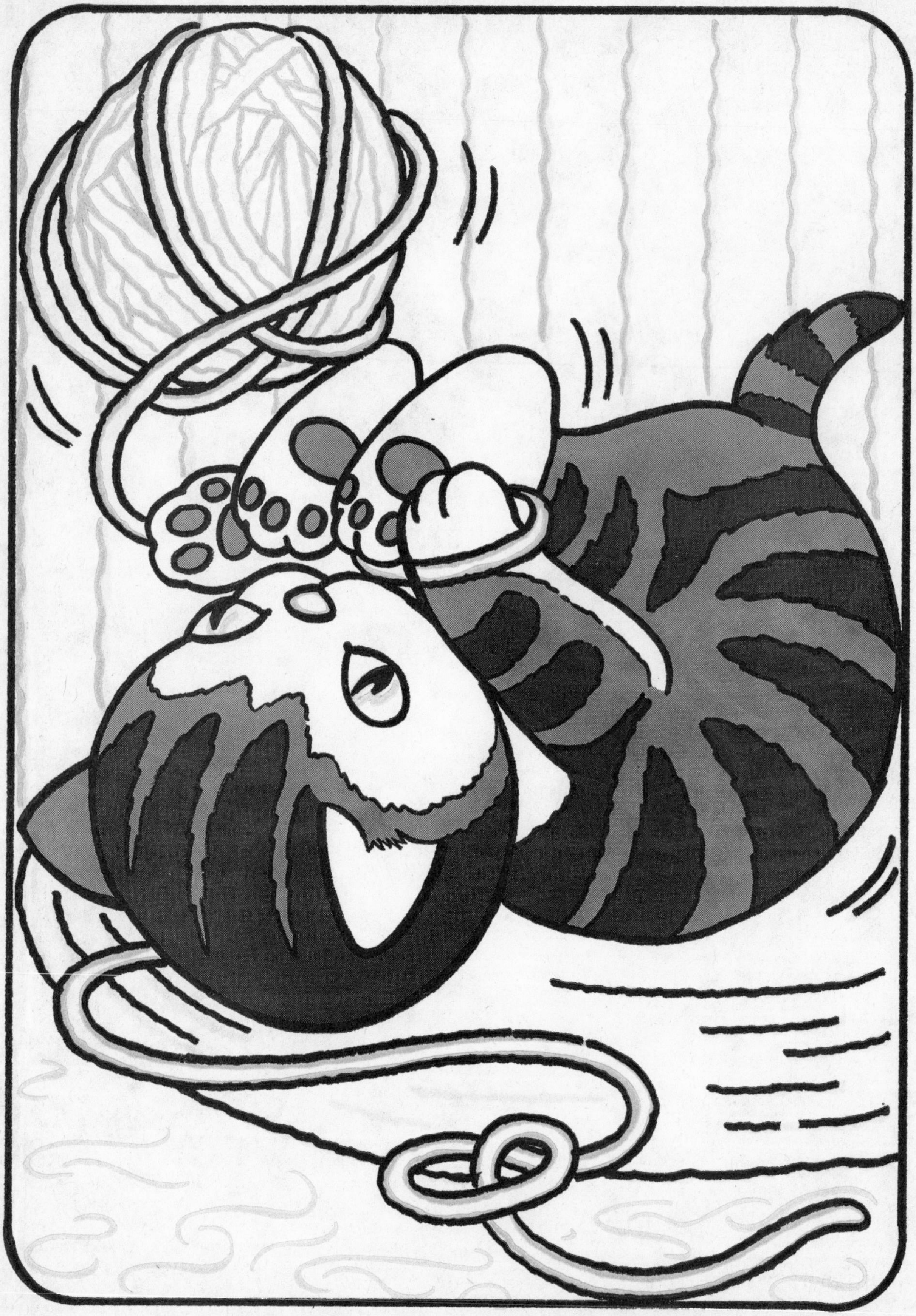

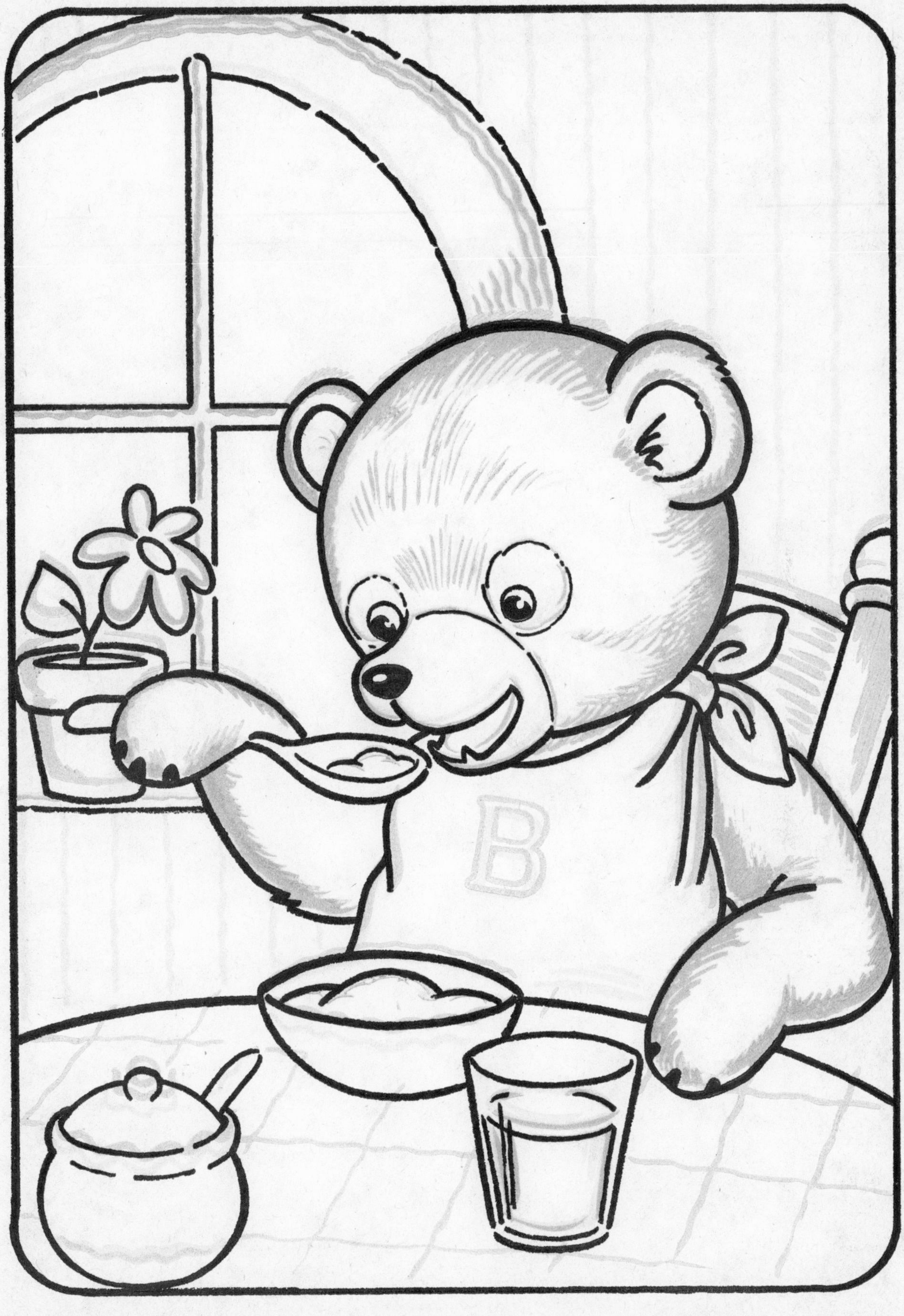
B

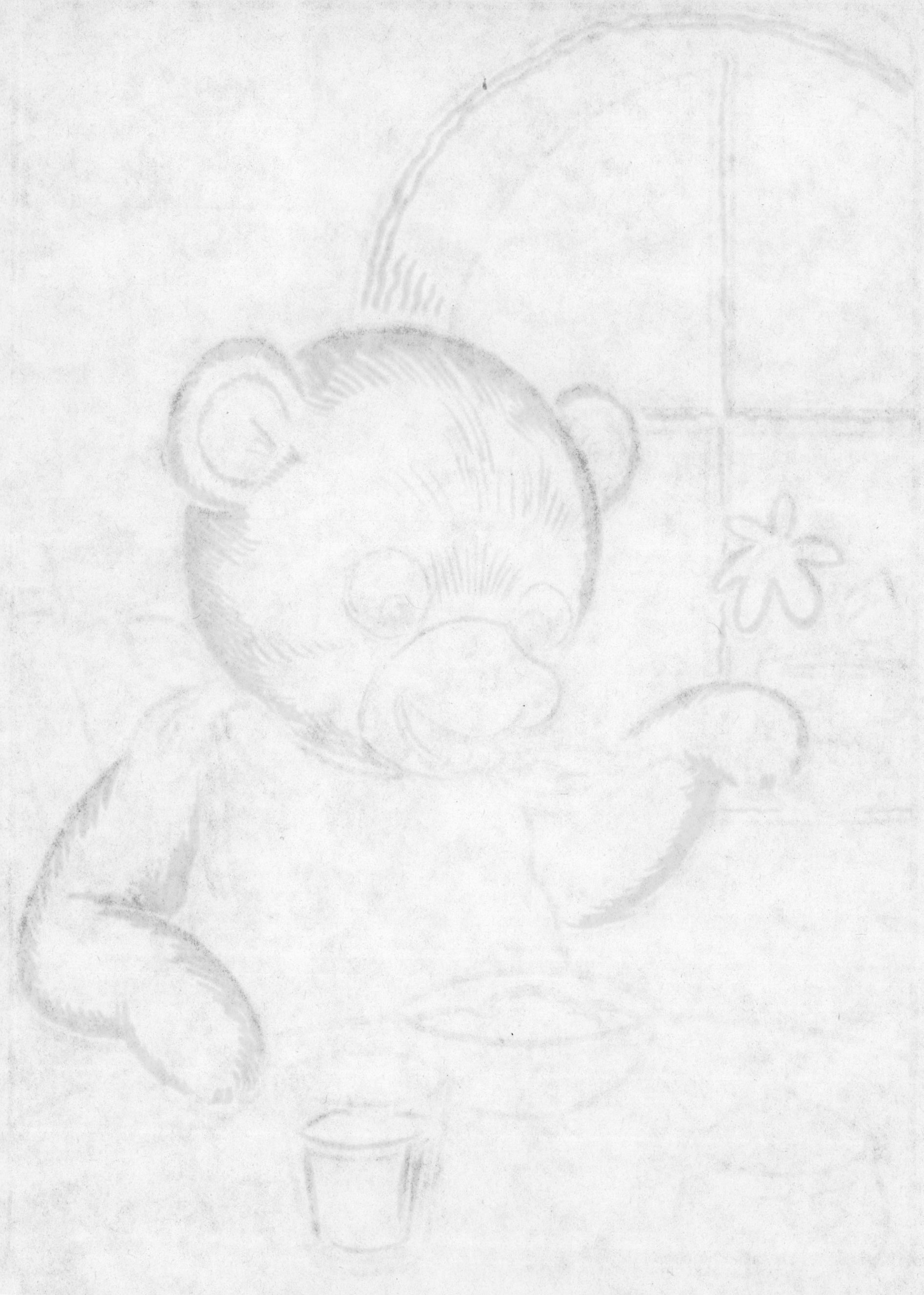

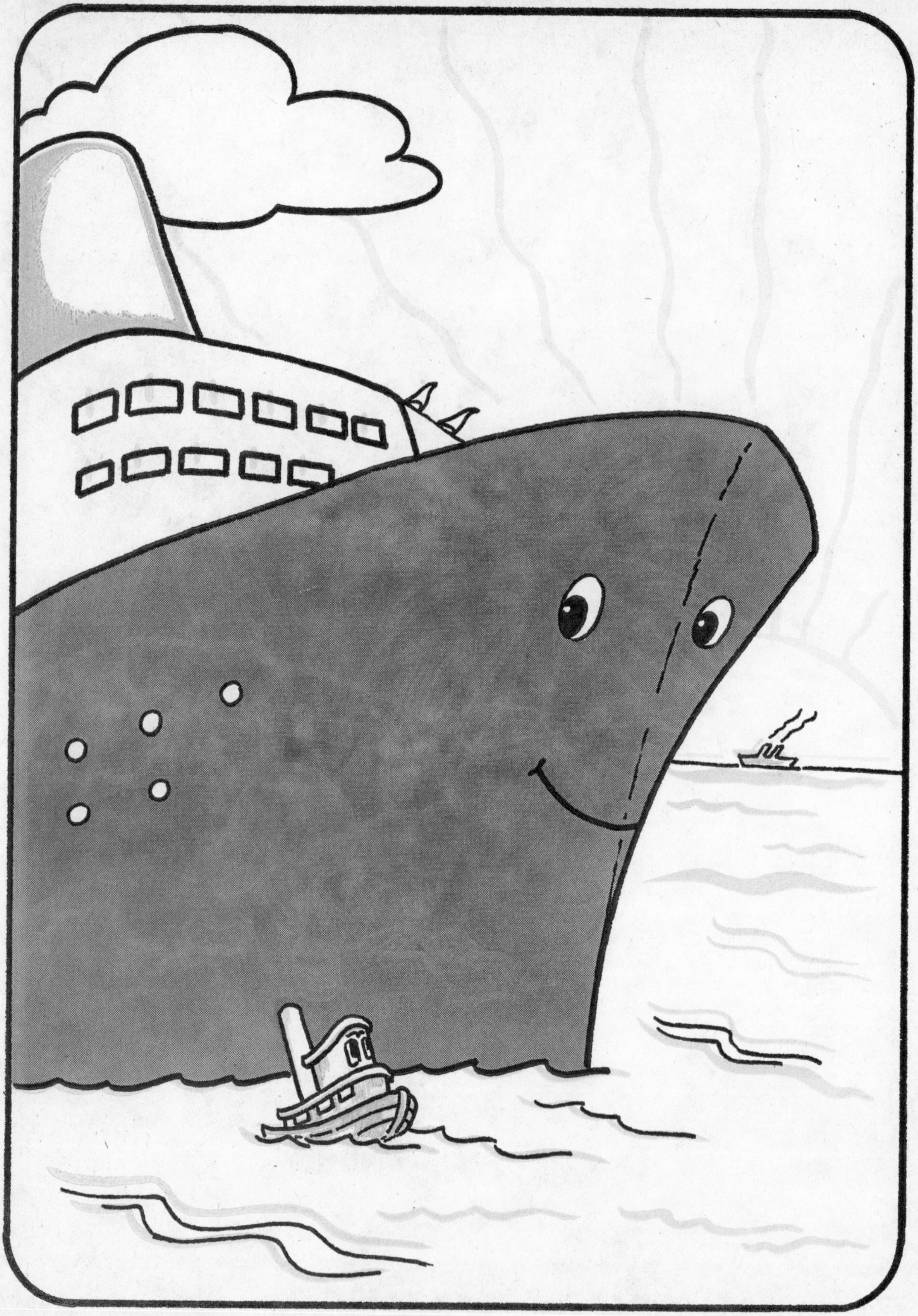

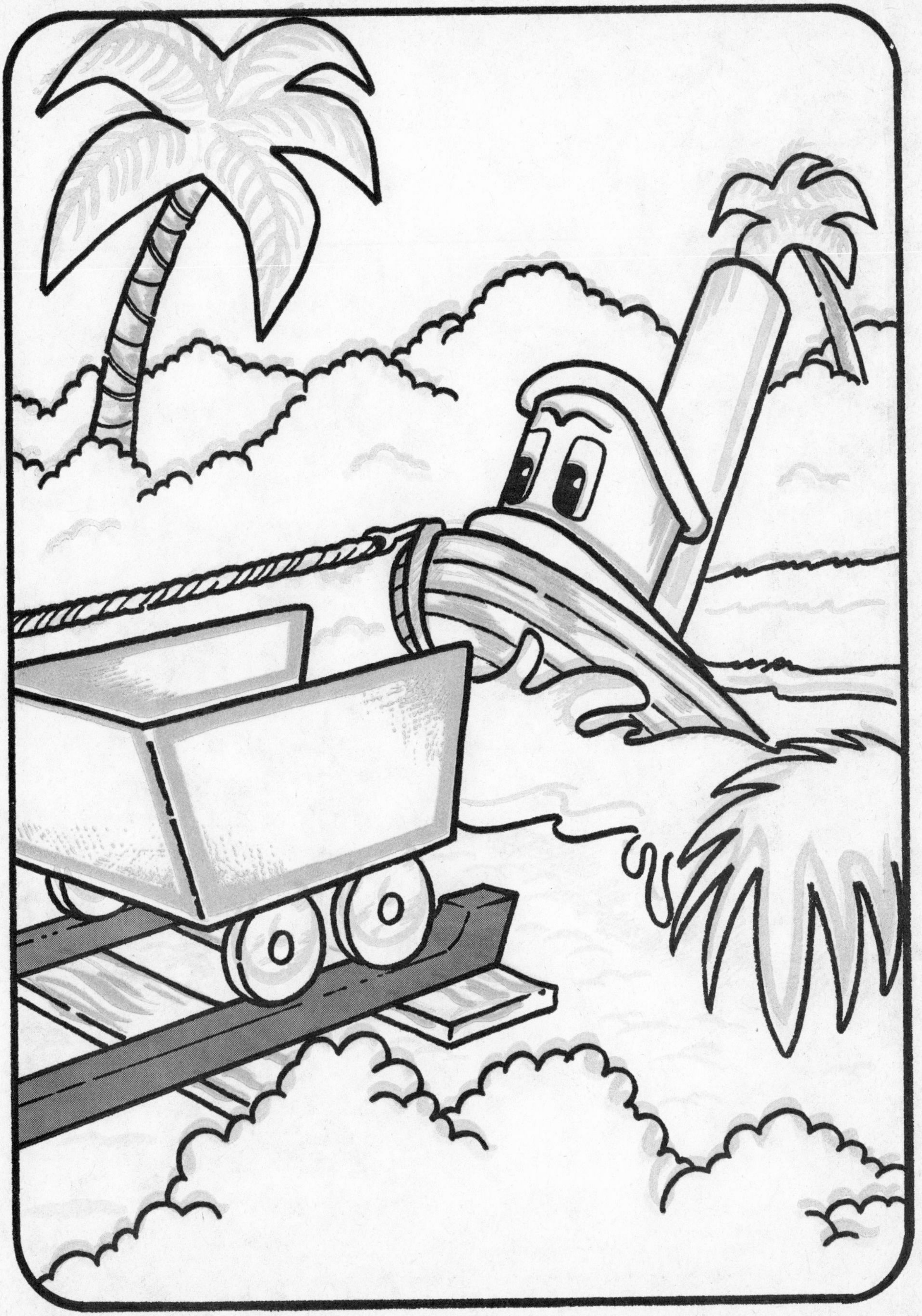

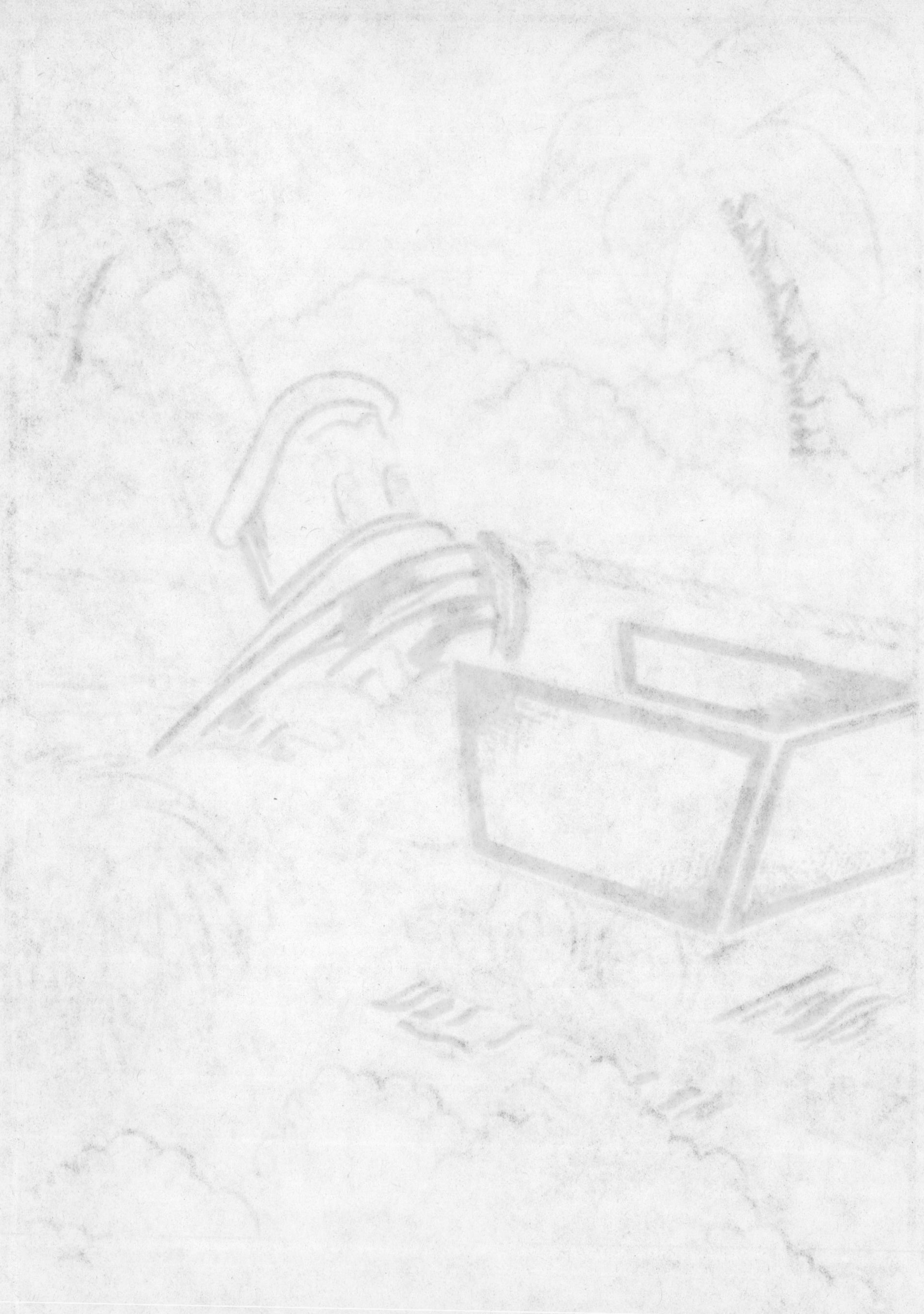

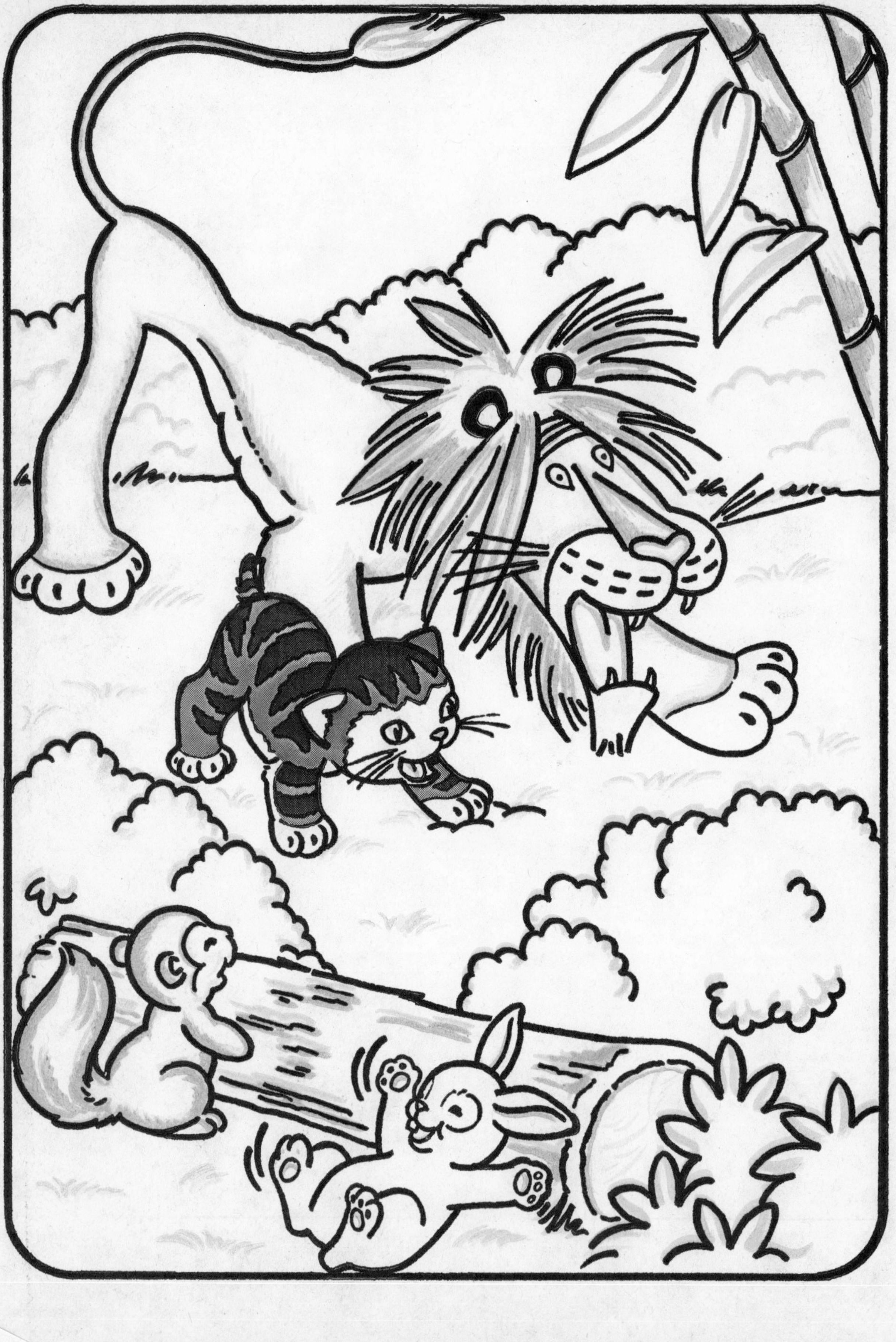

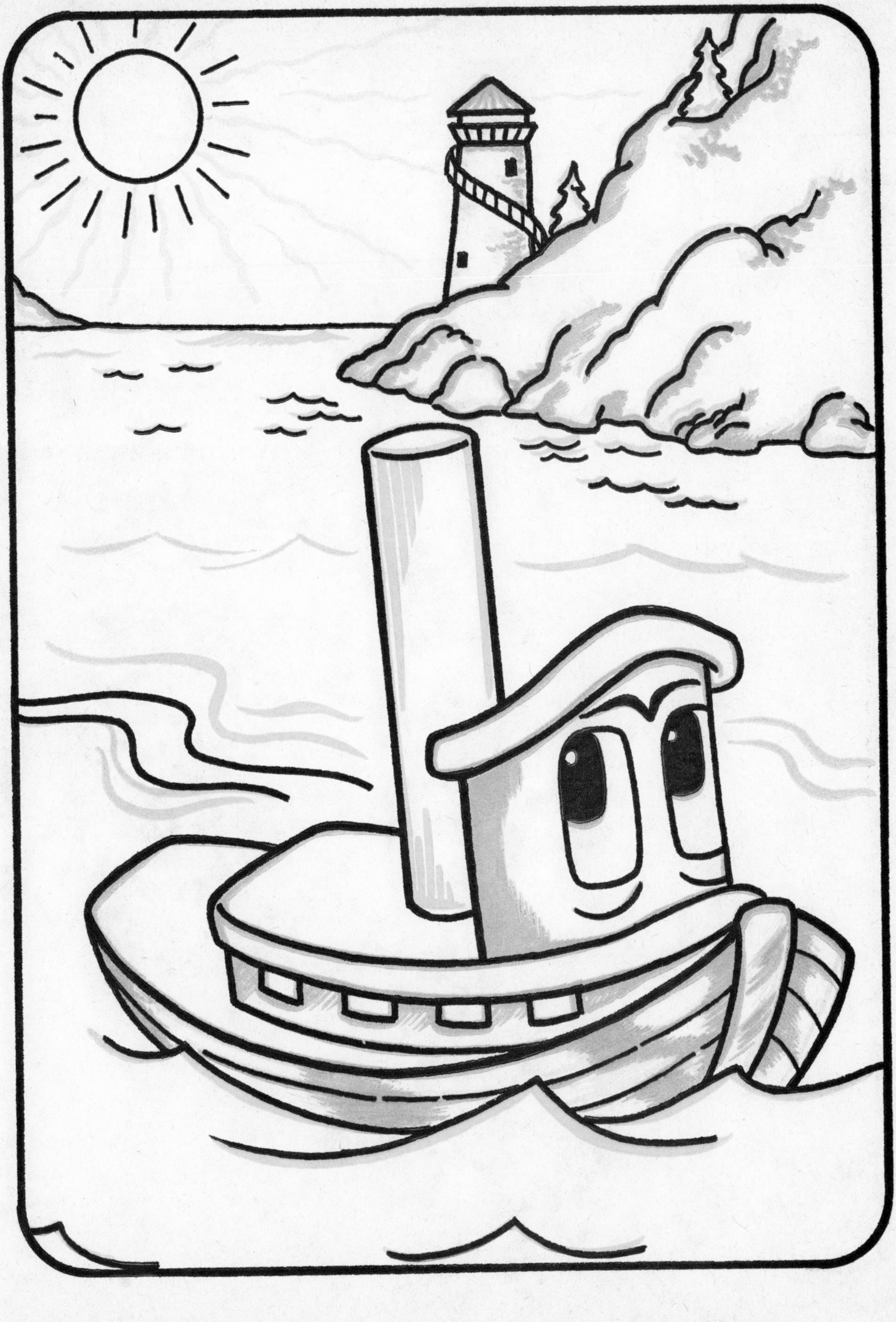

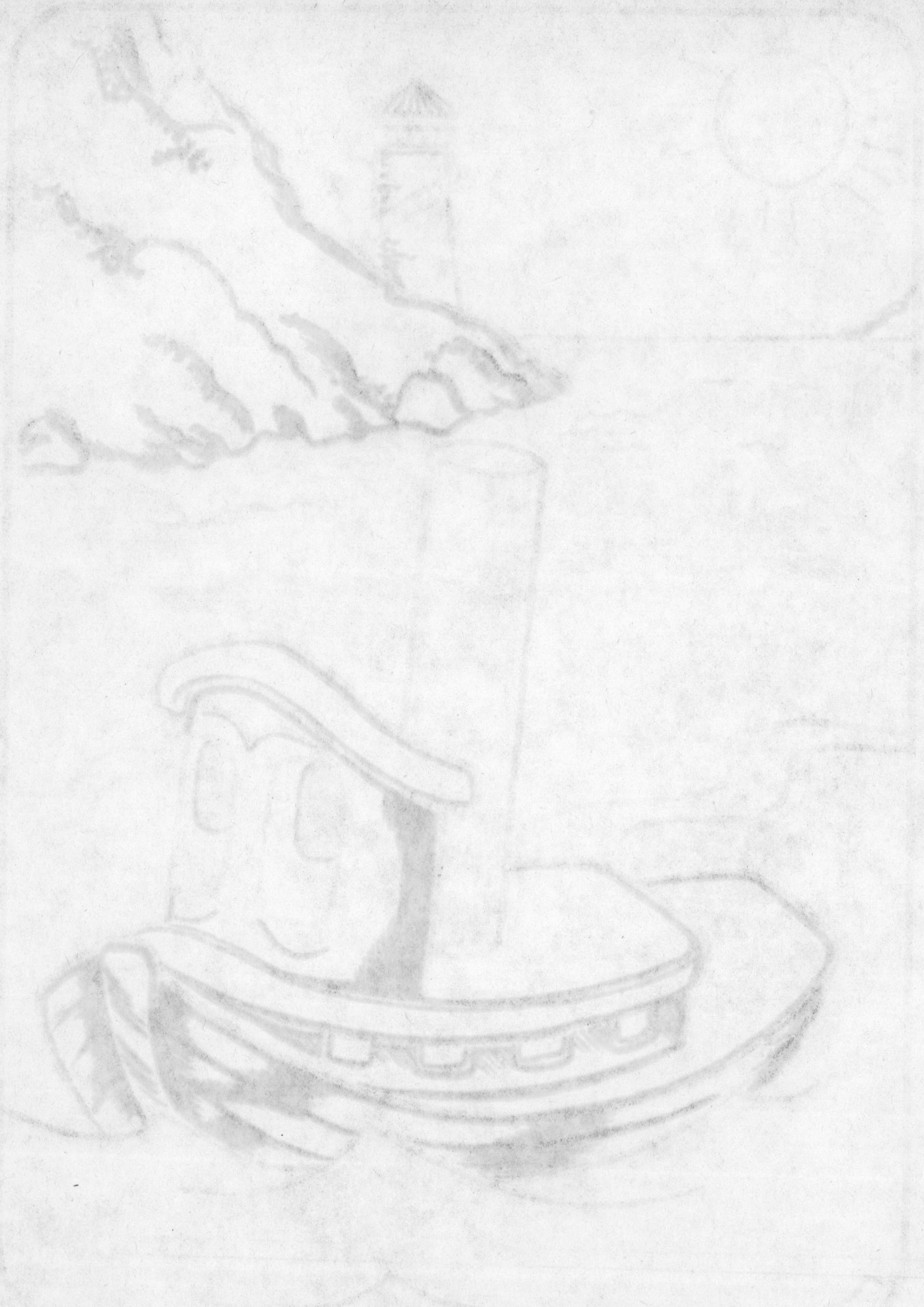

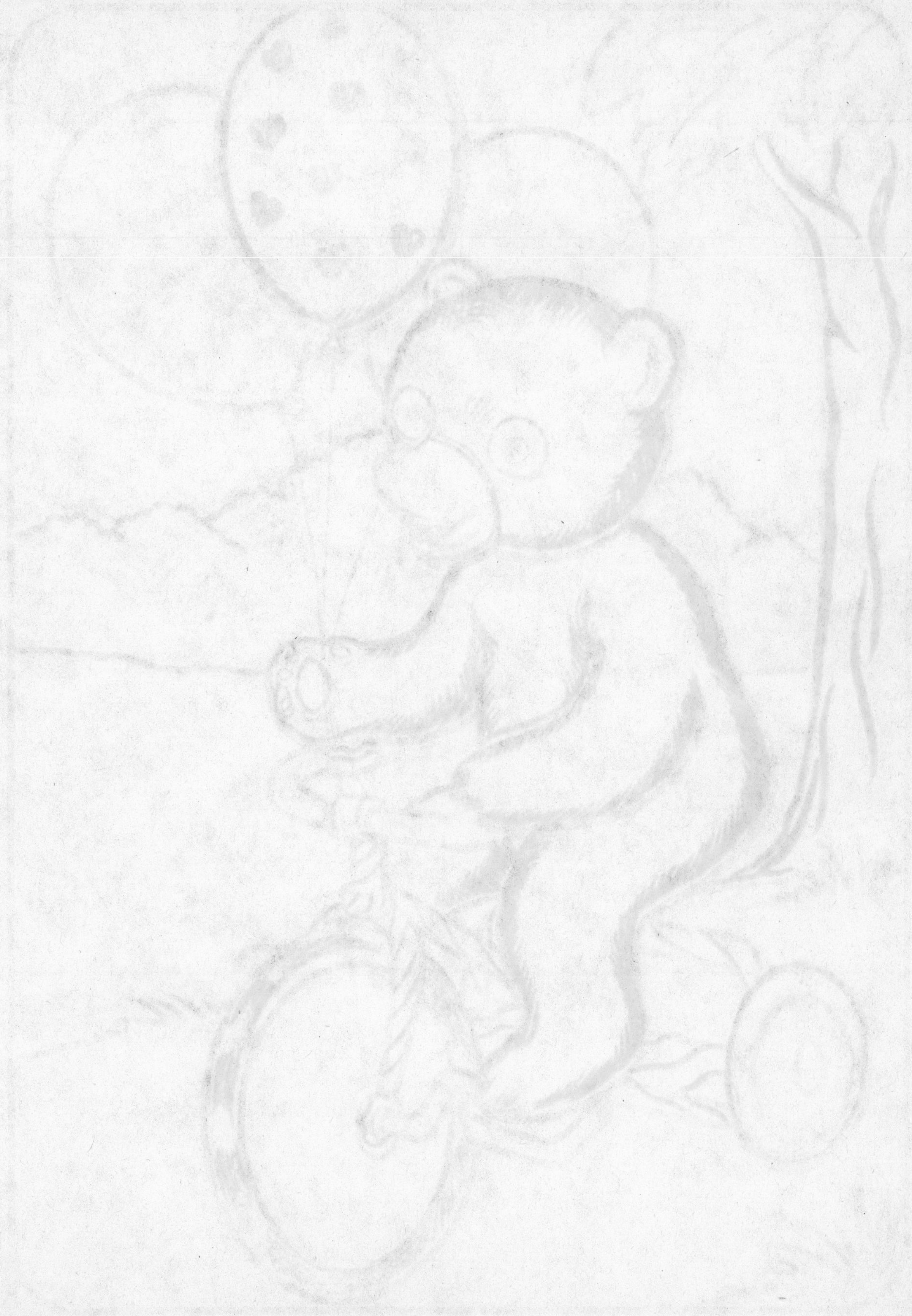

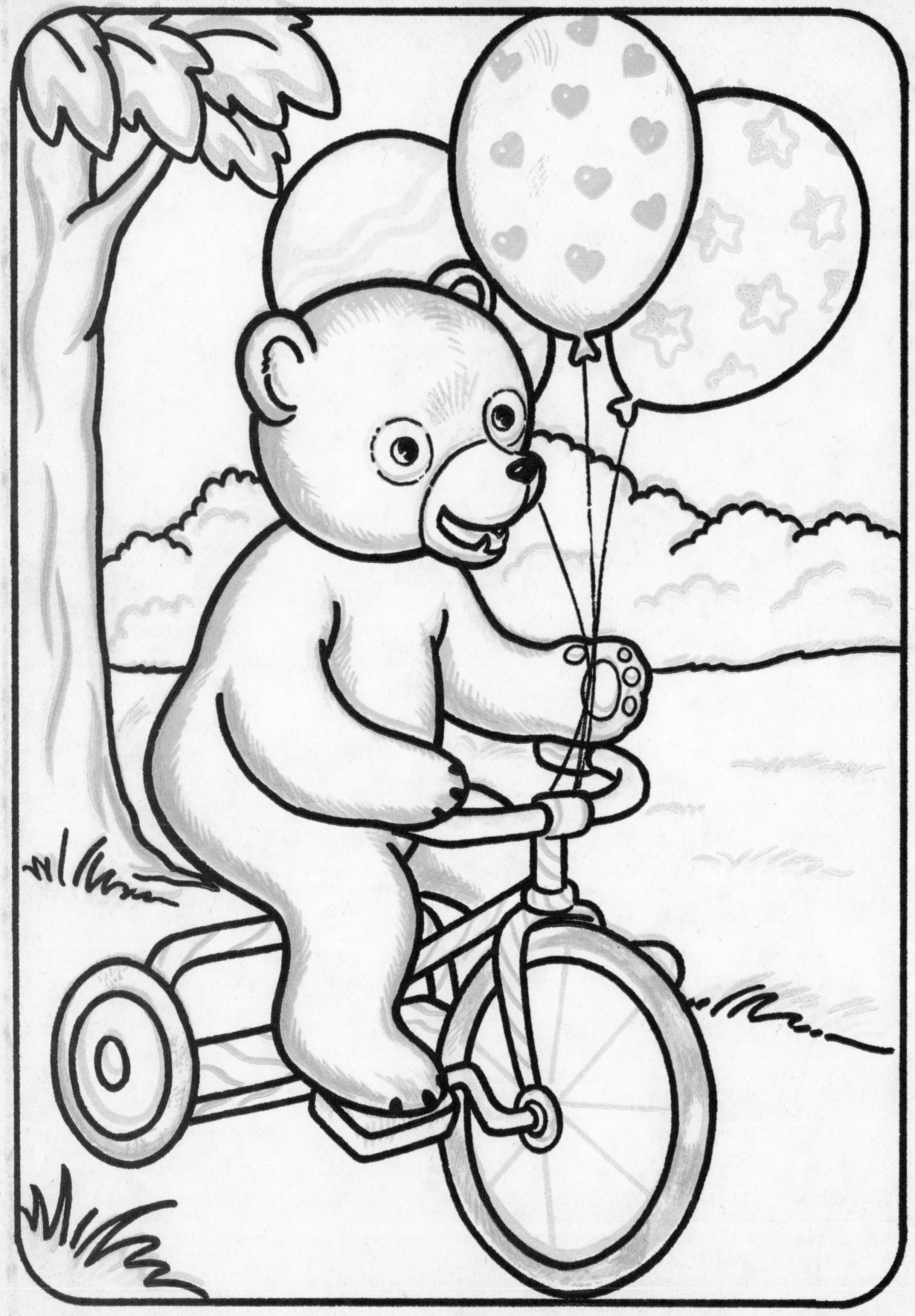

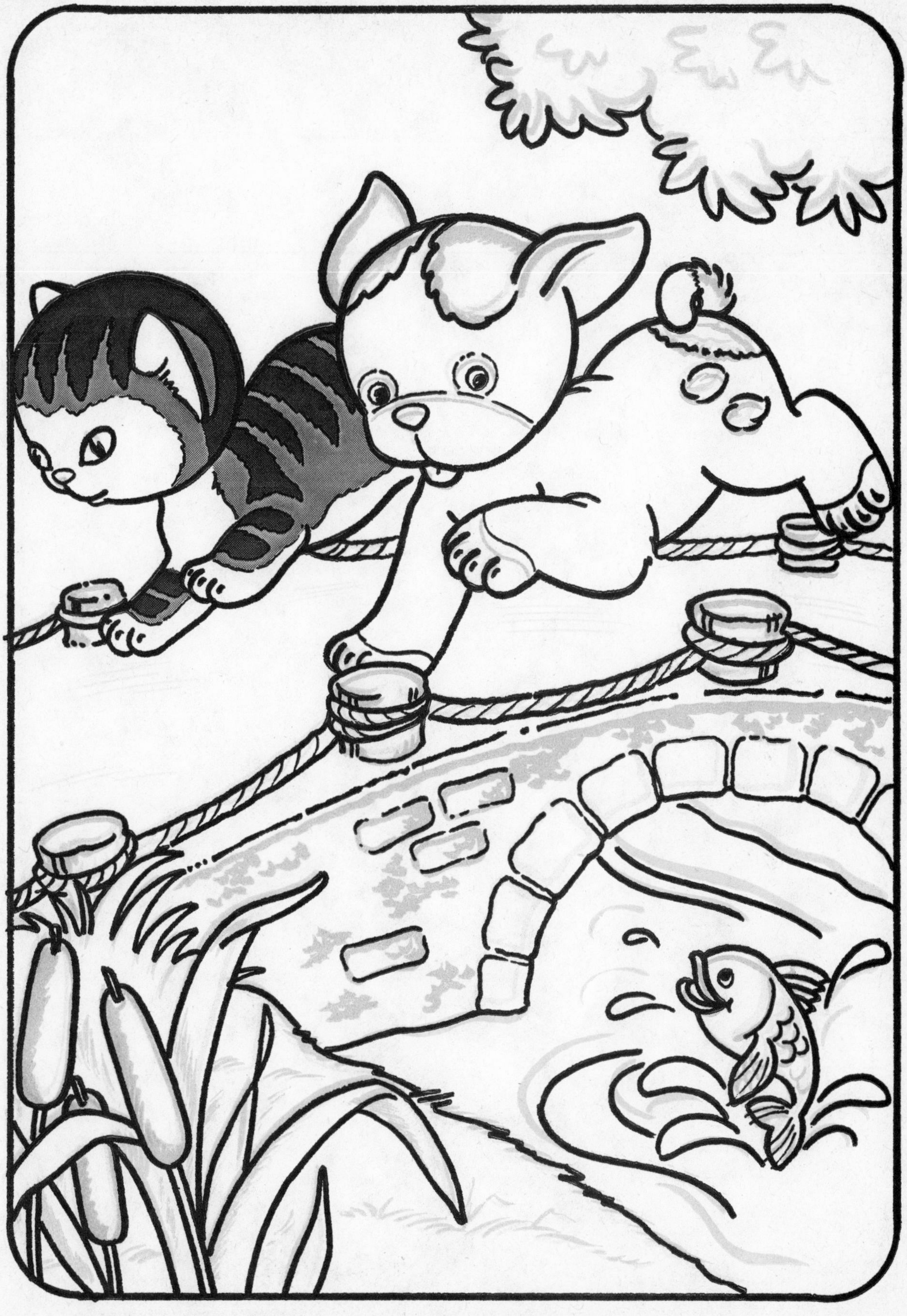

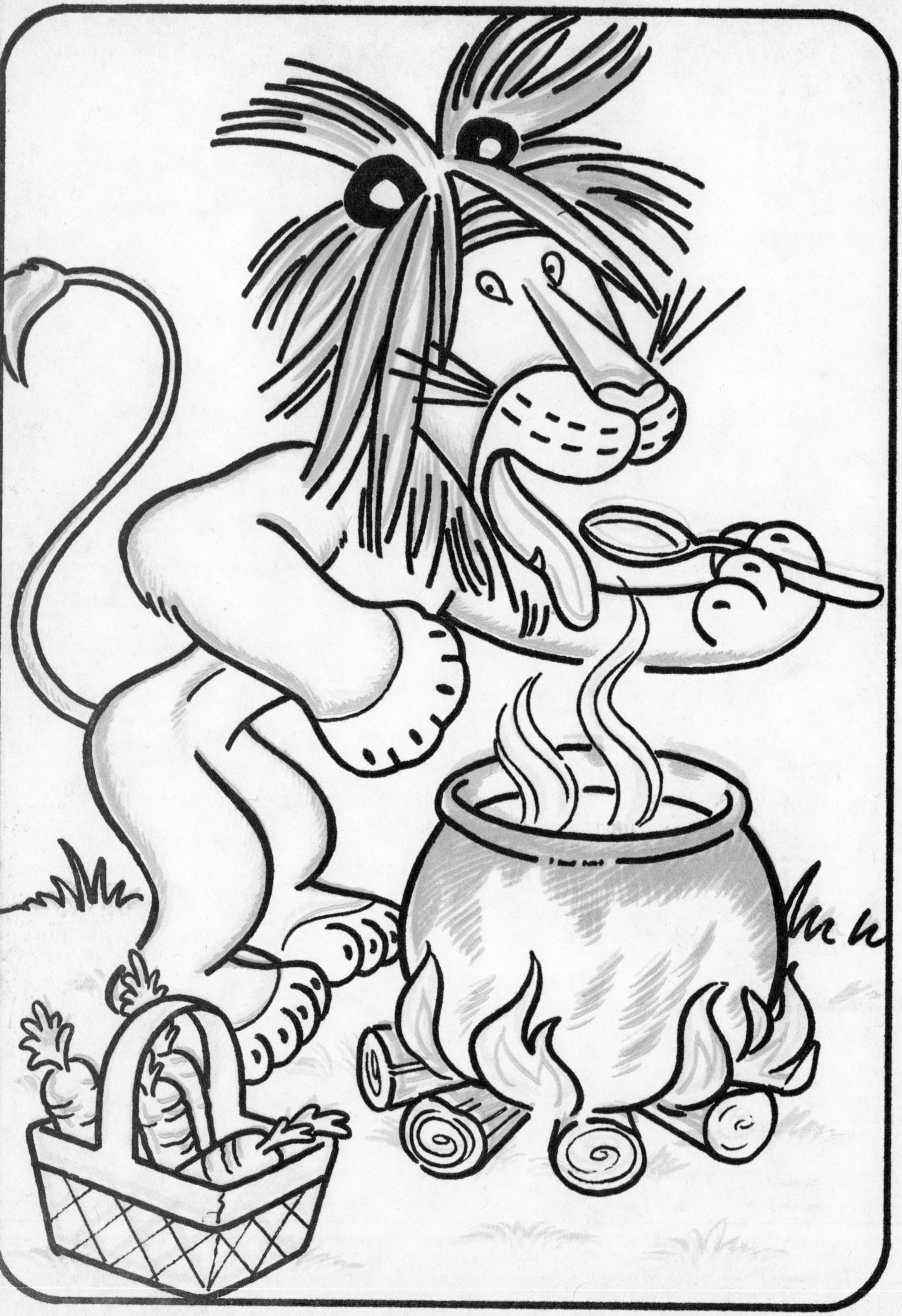

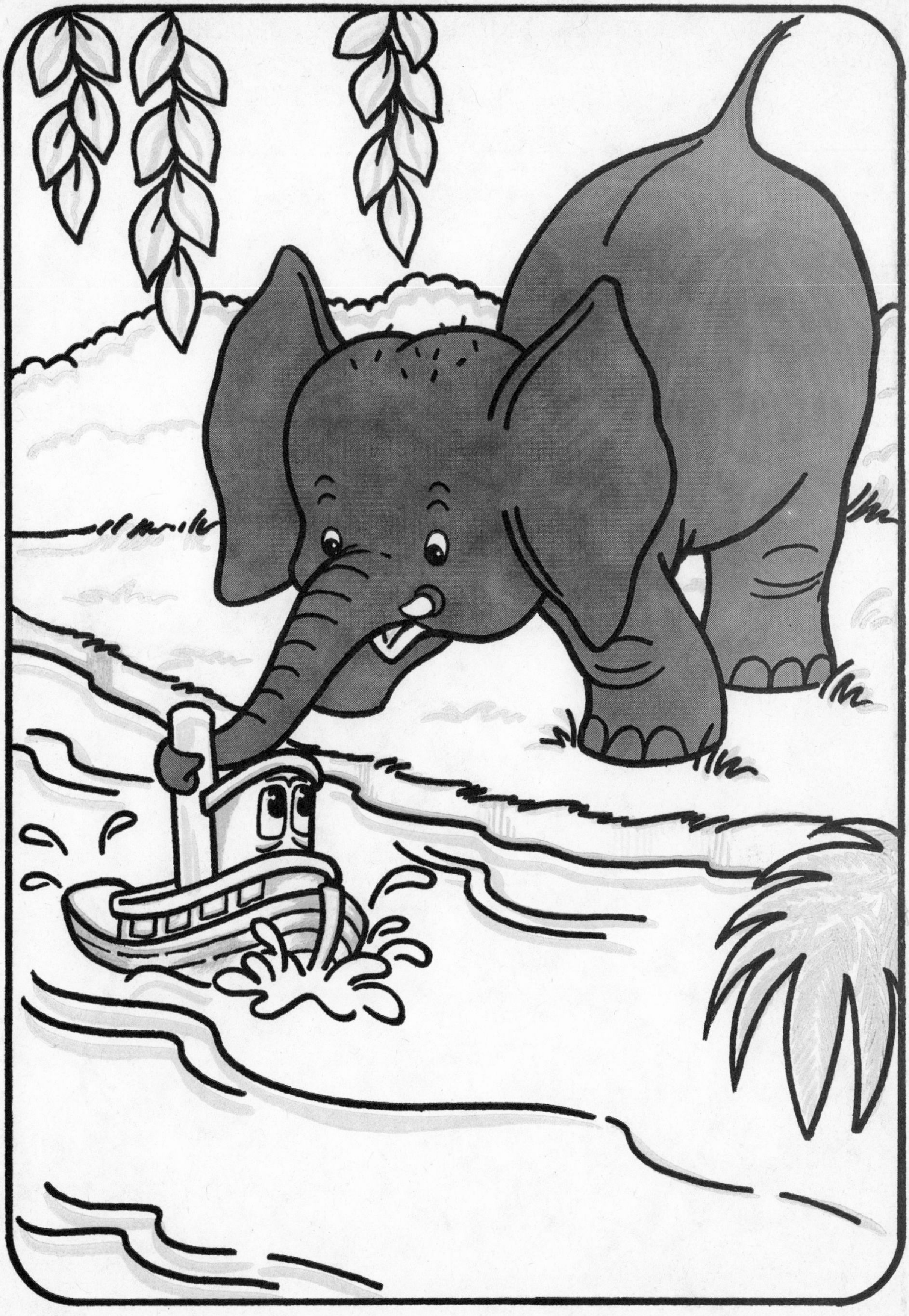

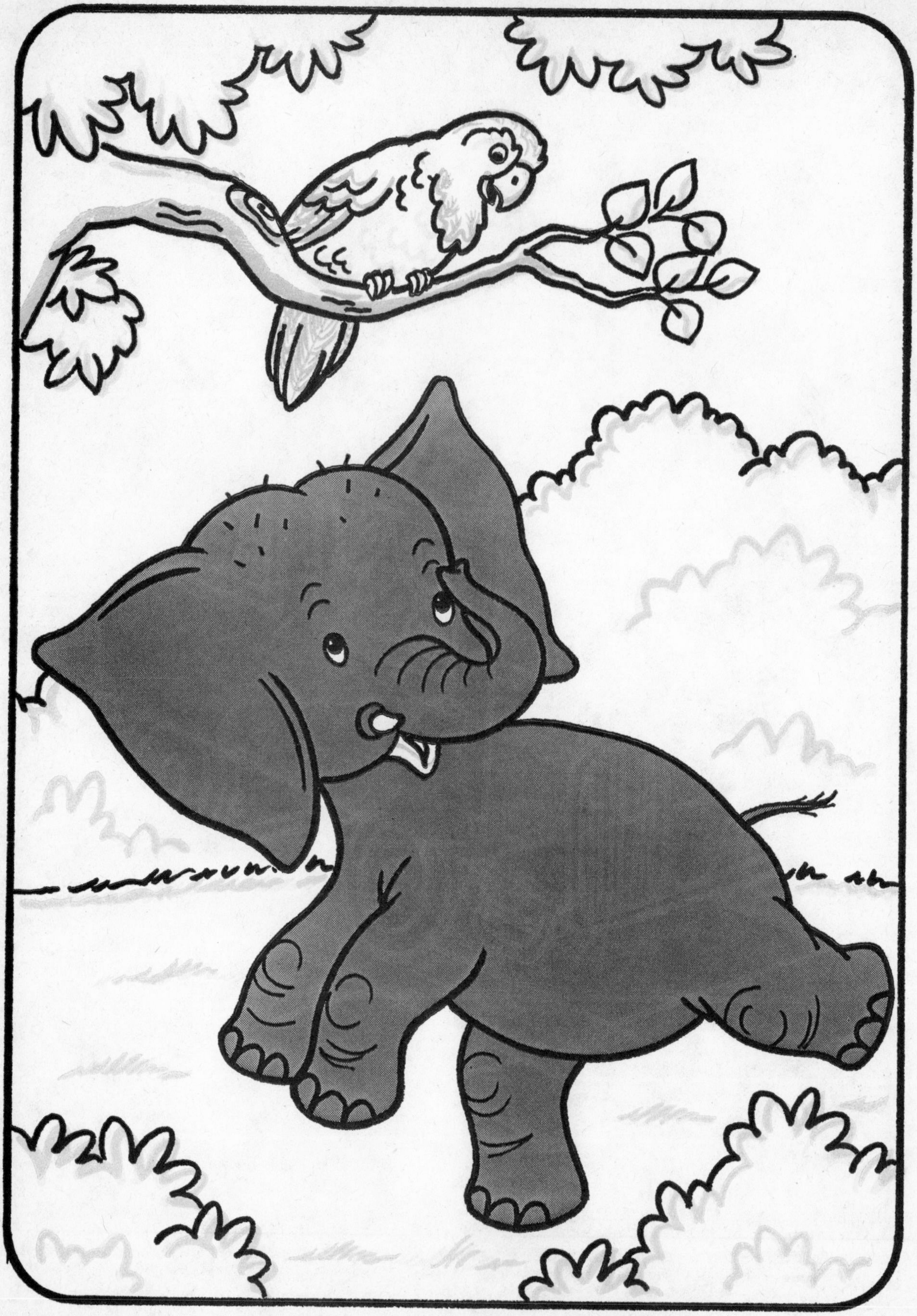

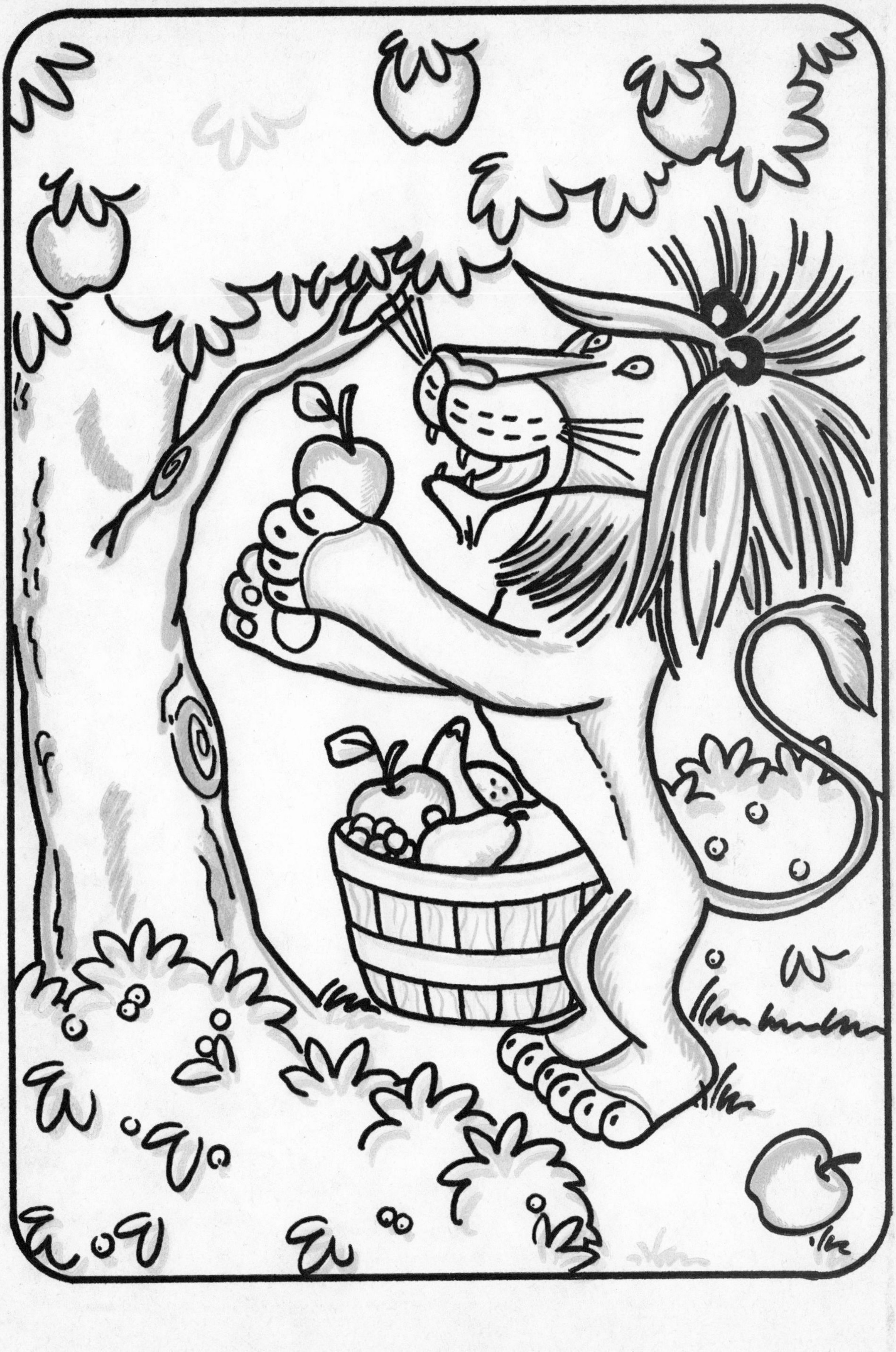

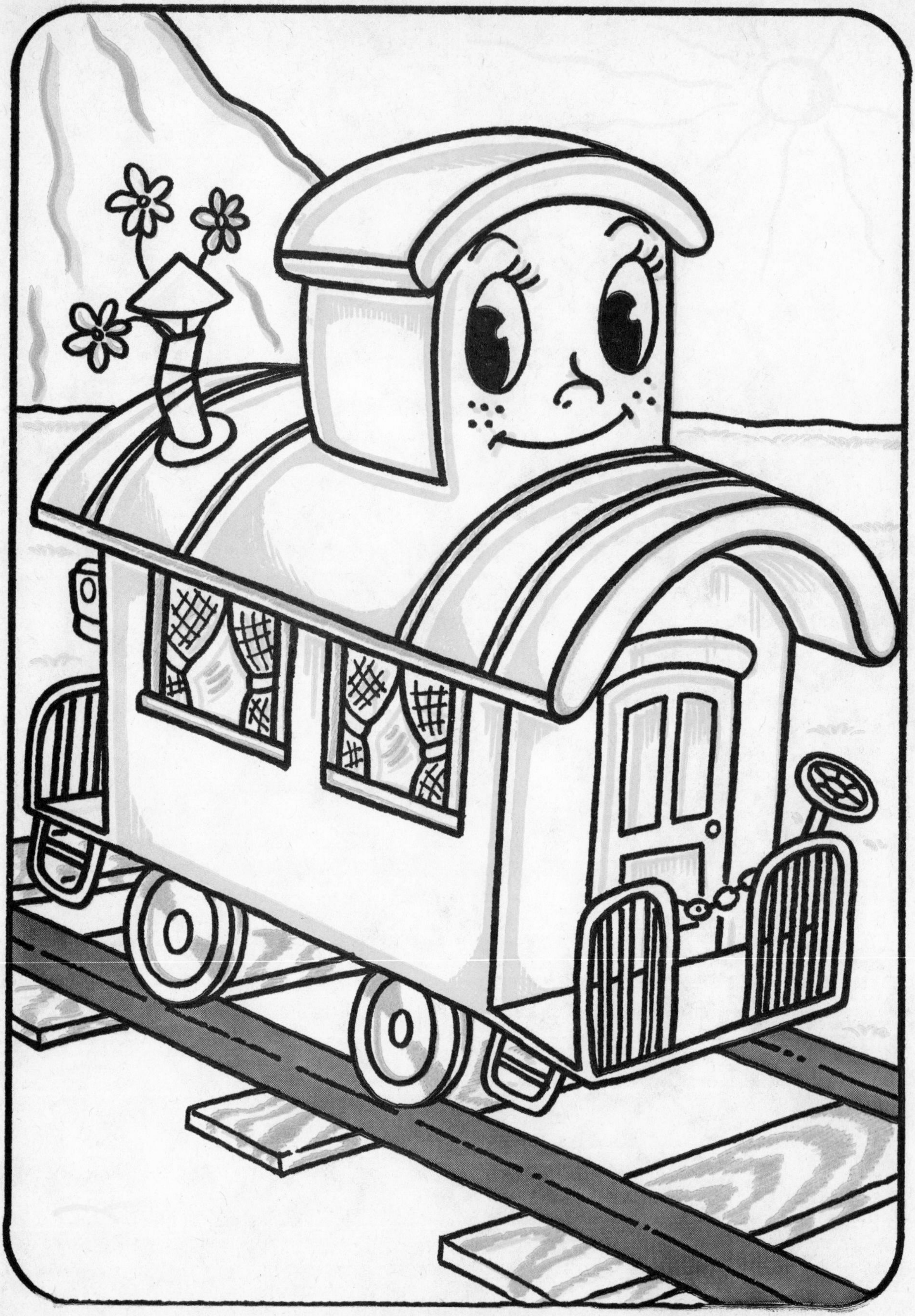

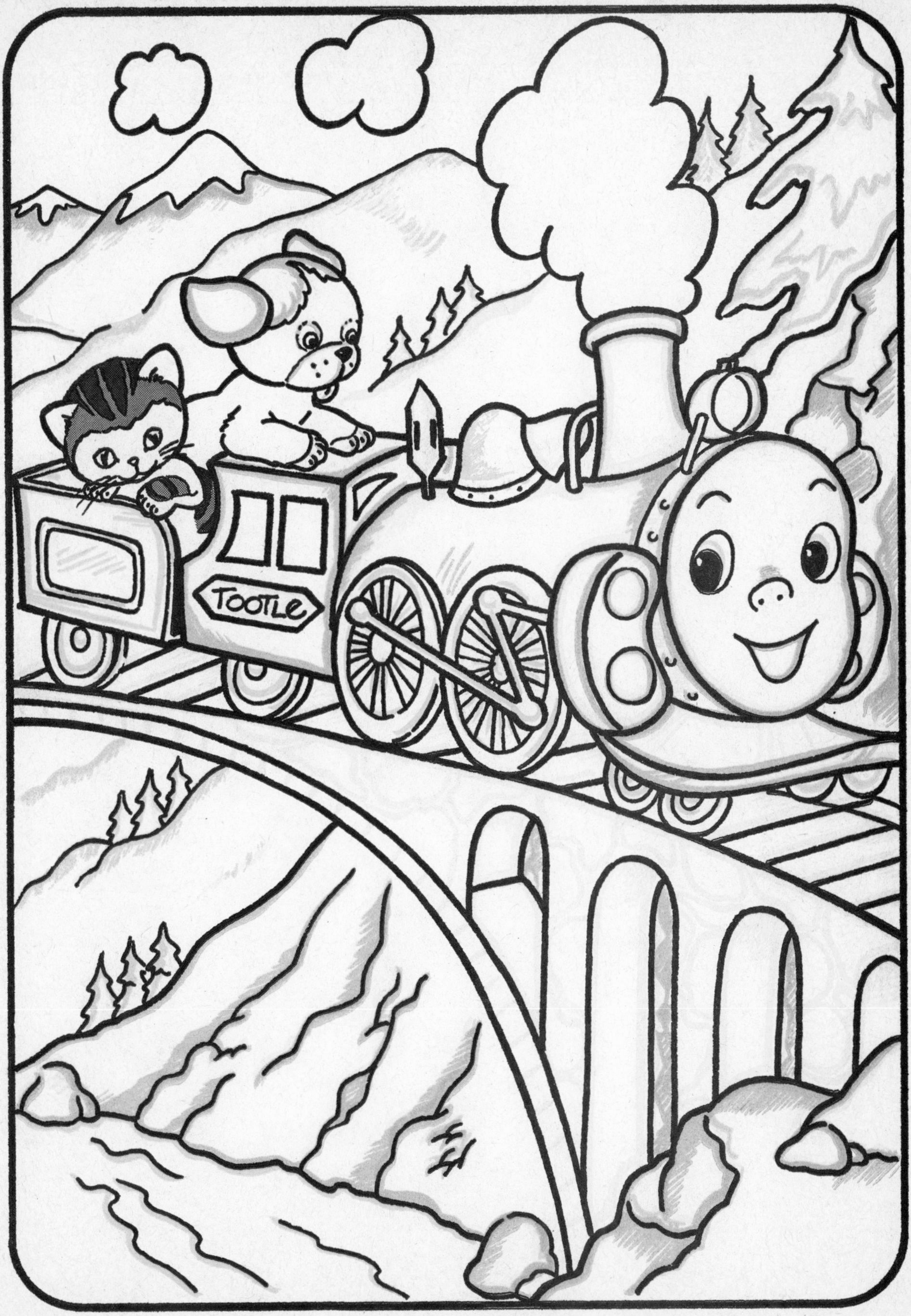
TOOTLE

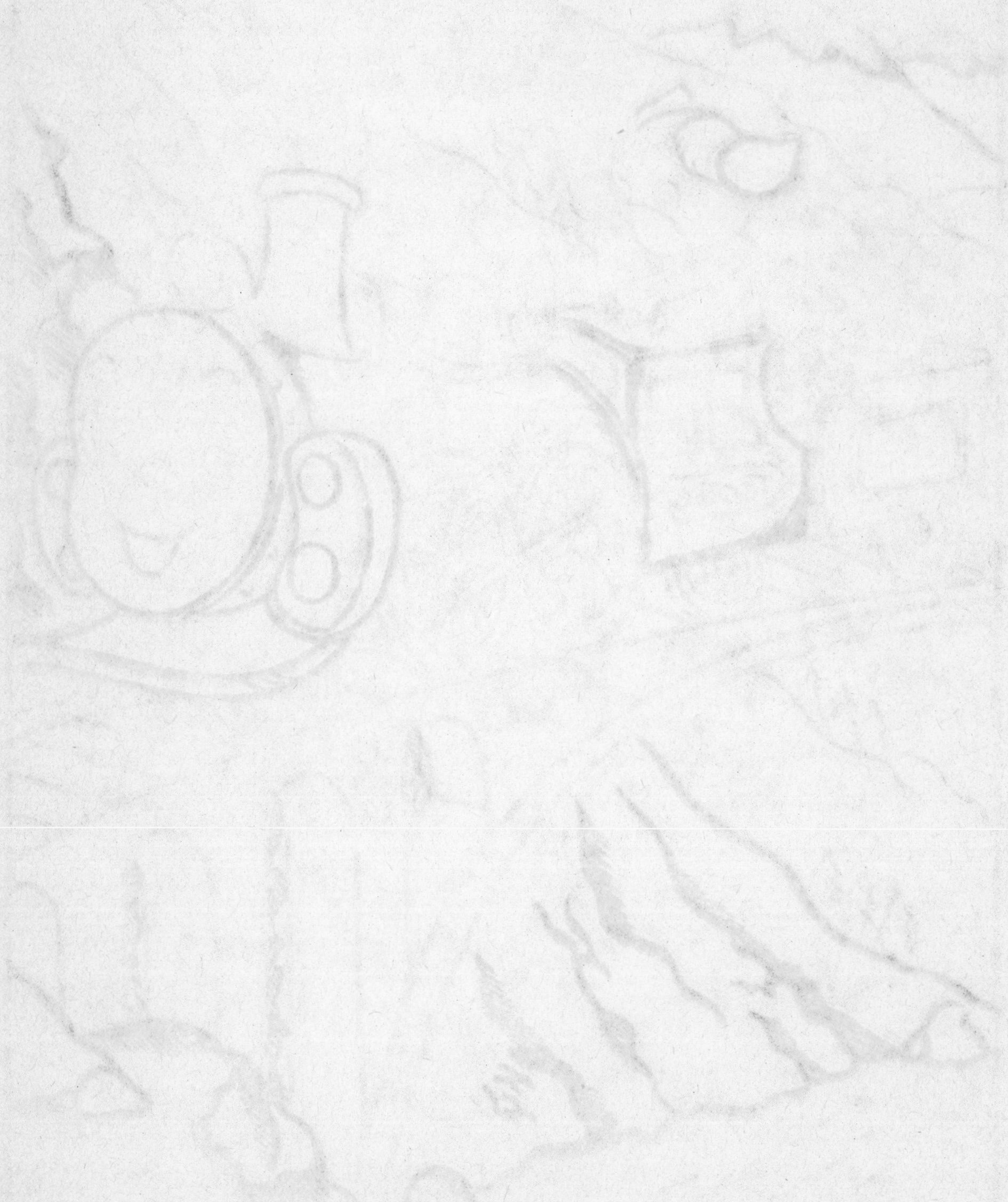

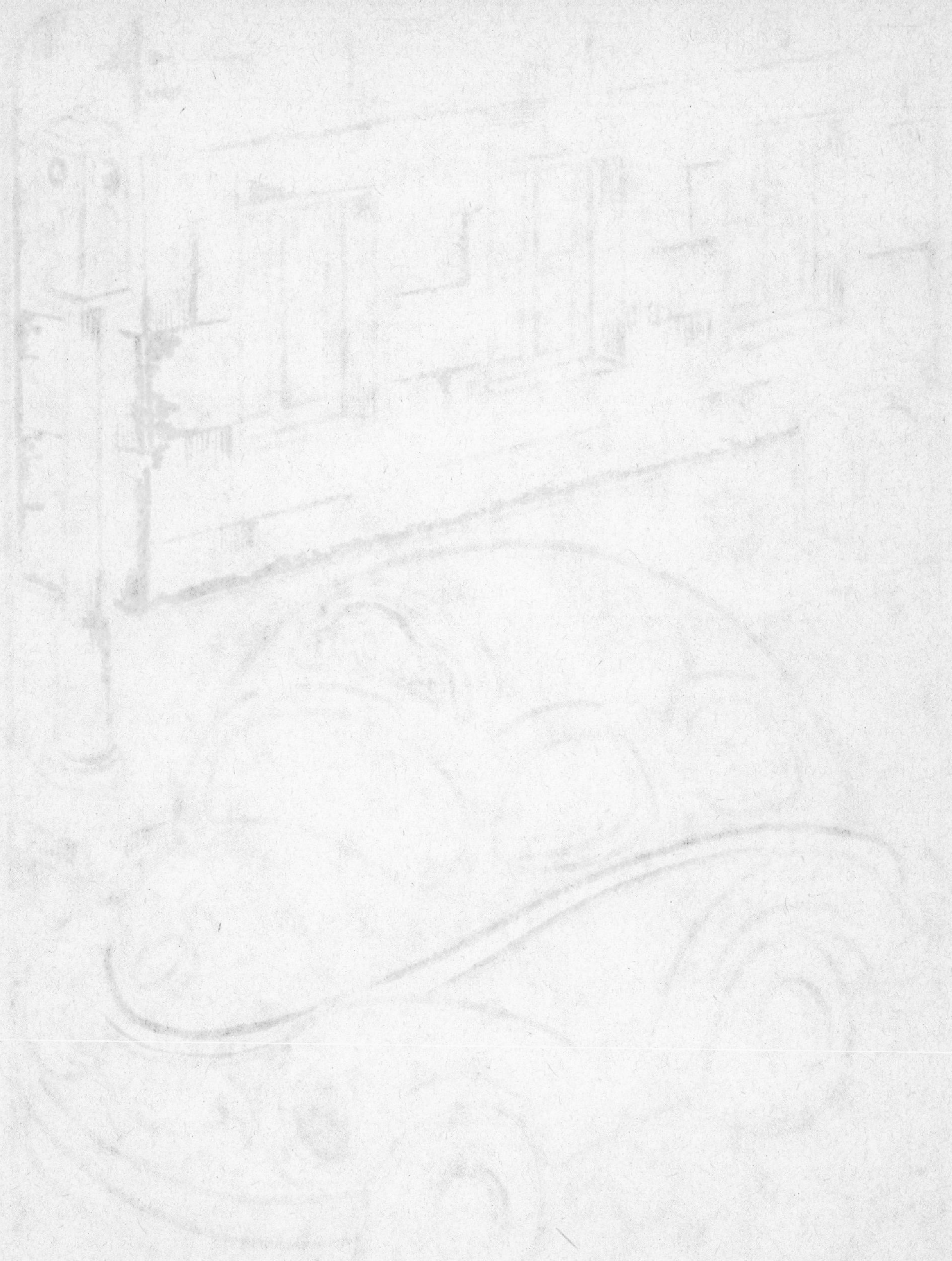

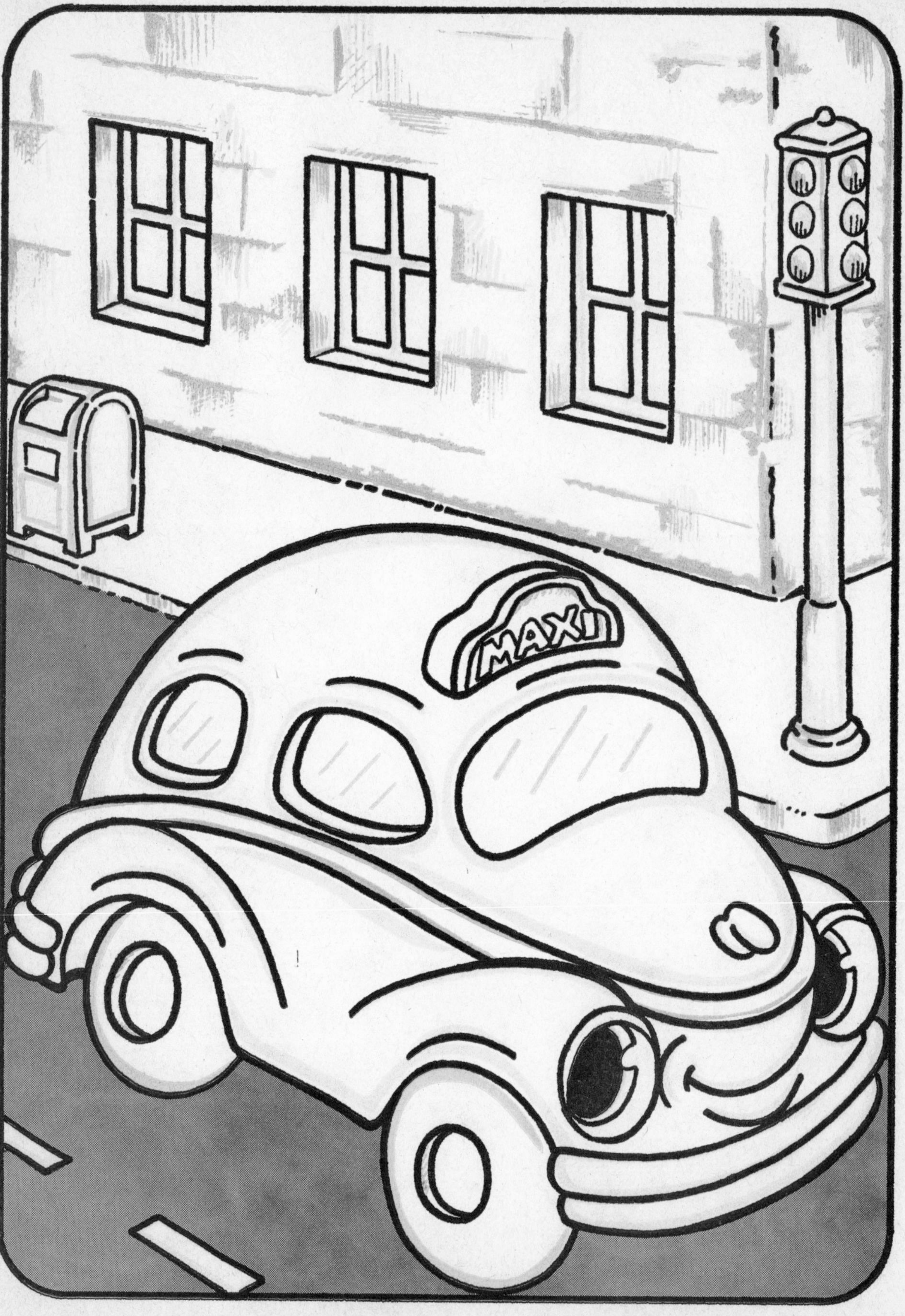
MAXI

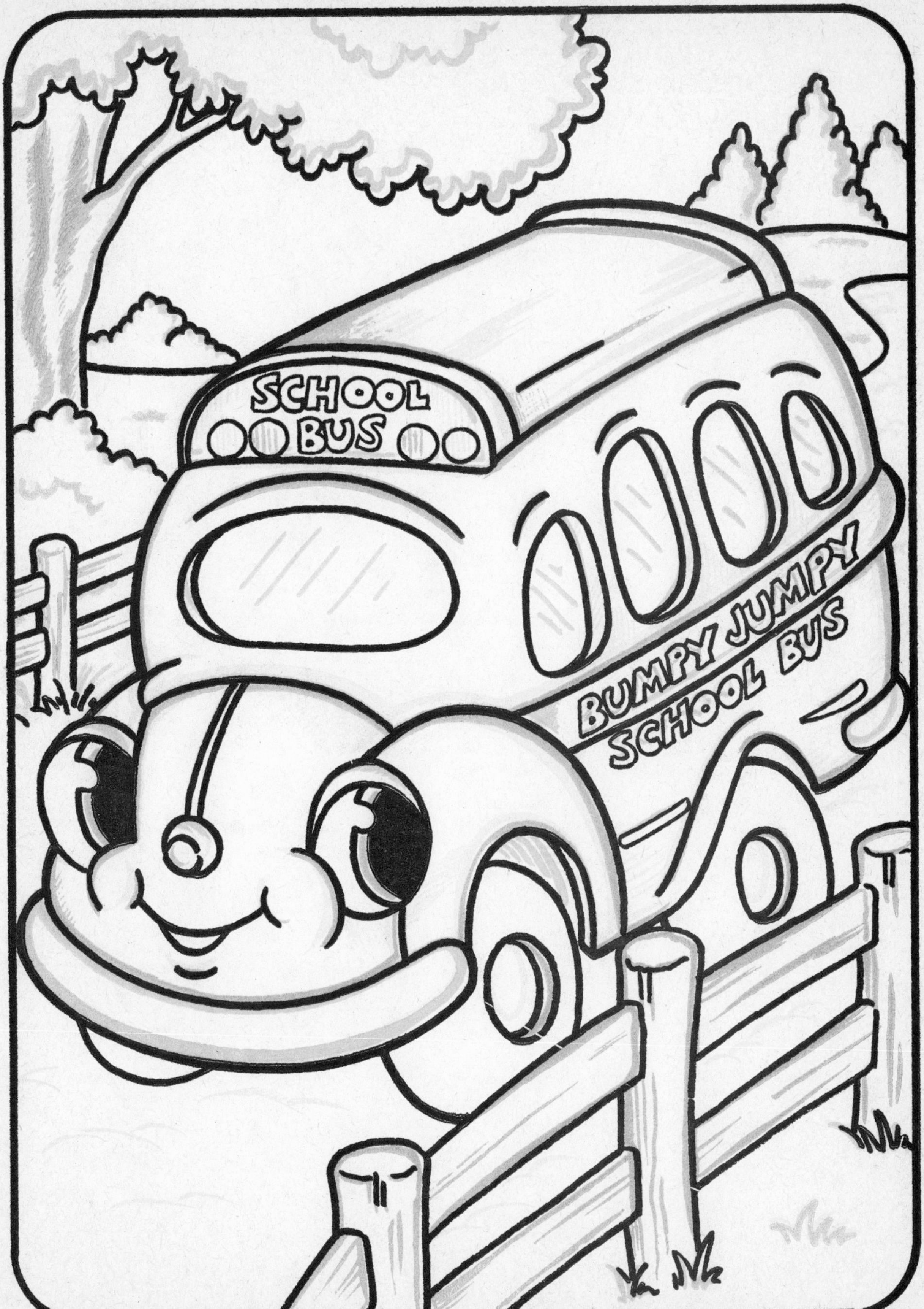
SCHOOL BUS
BUMPY JUMPY SCHOOL BUS

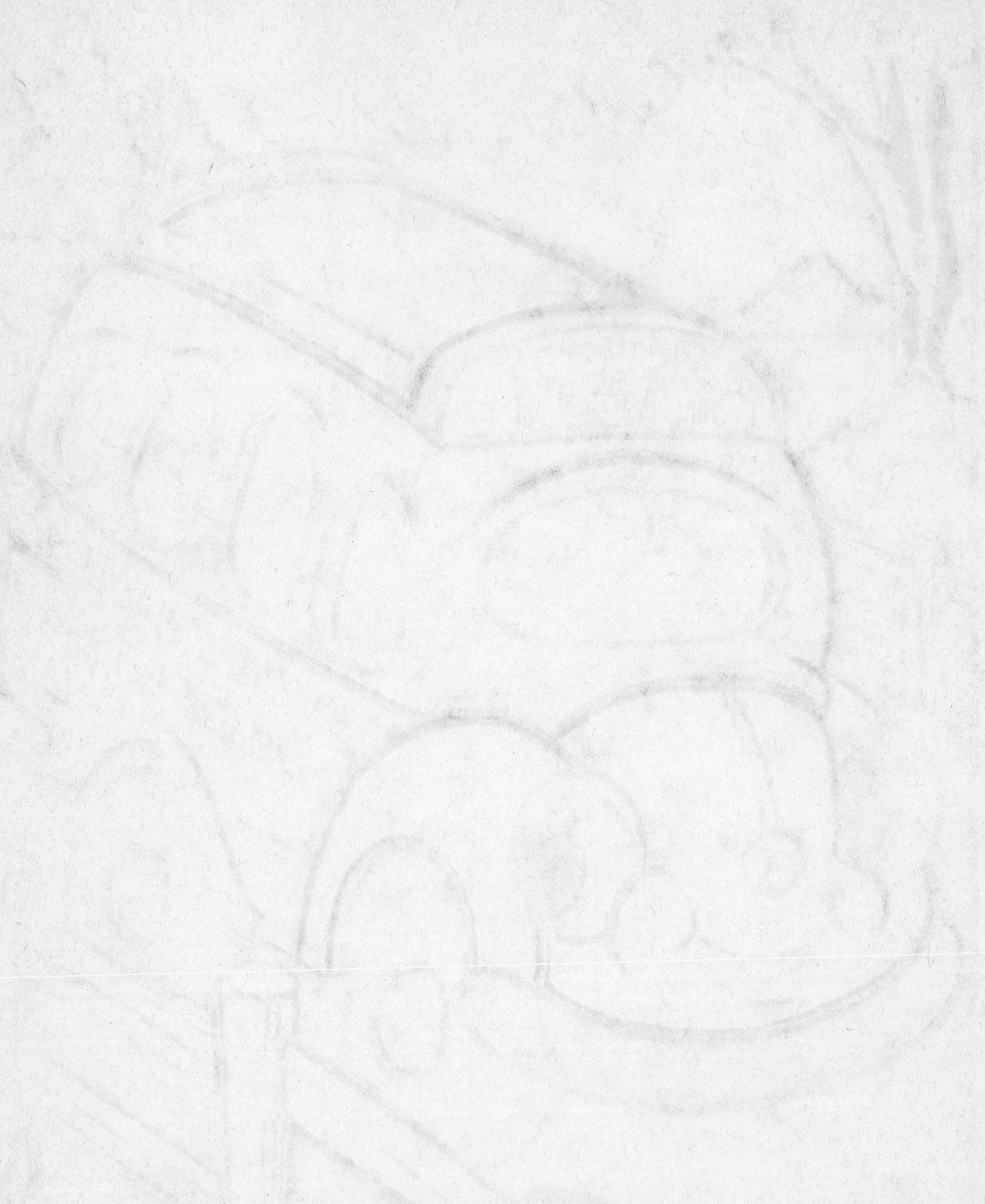

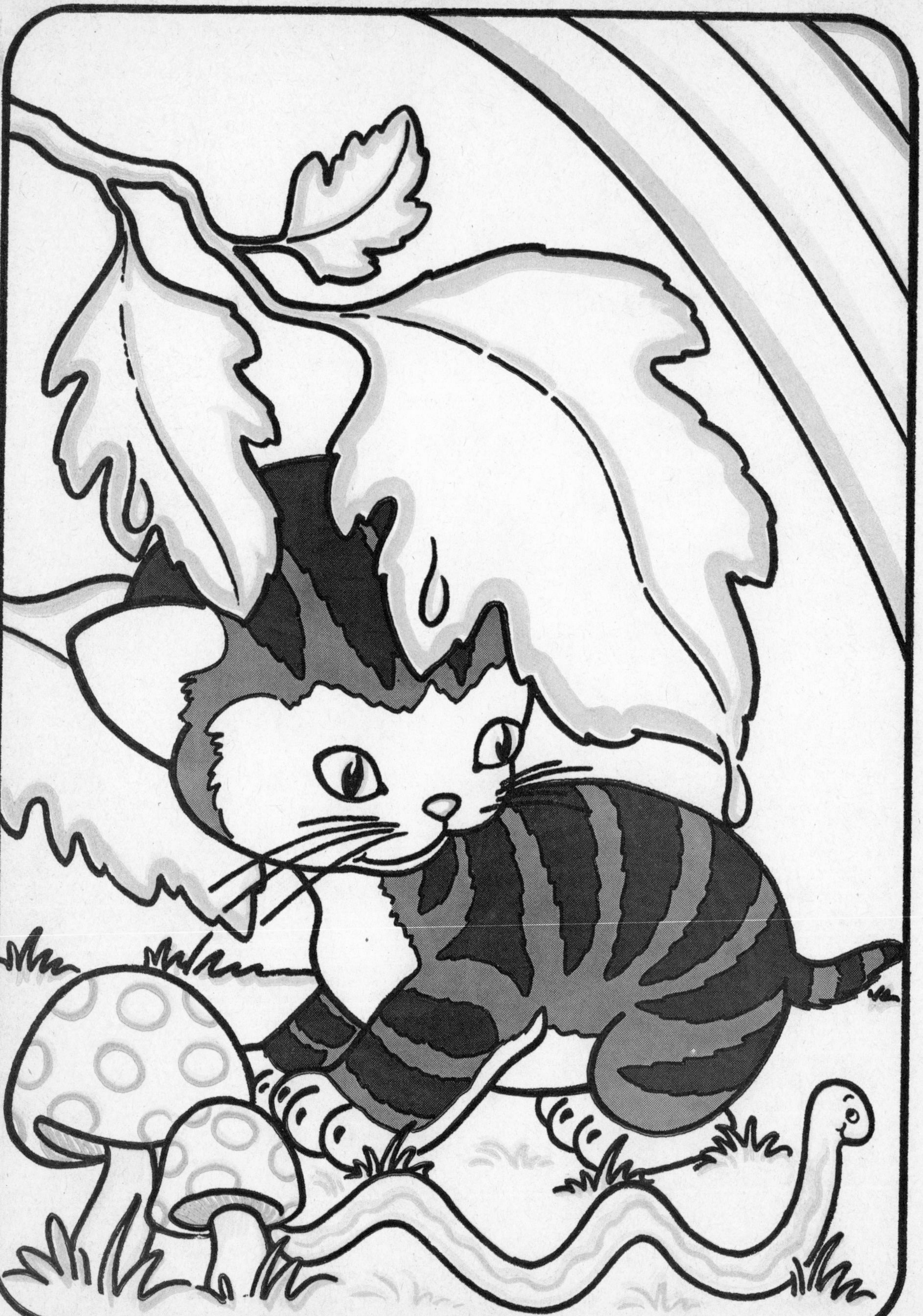

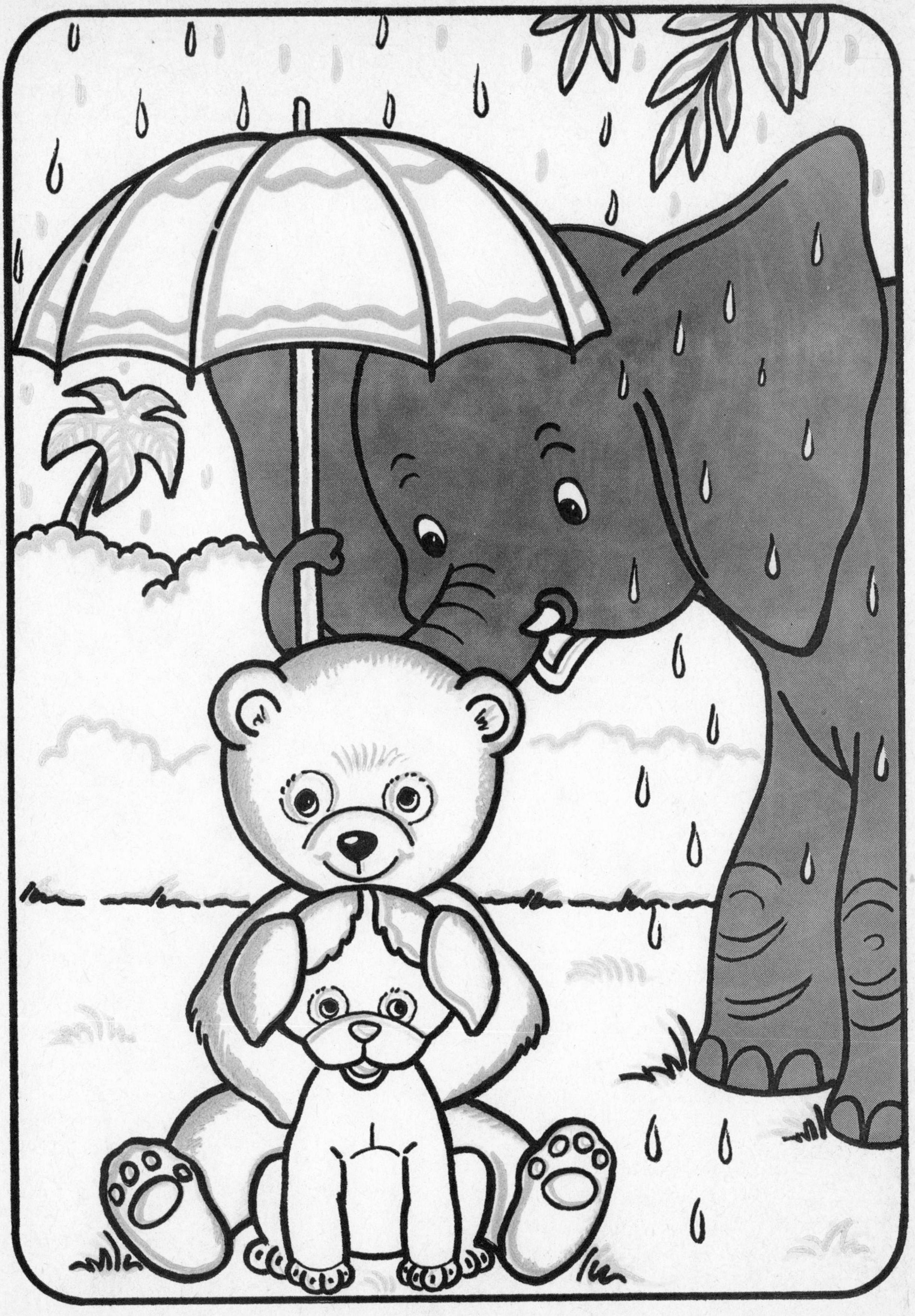

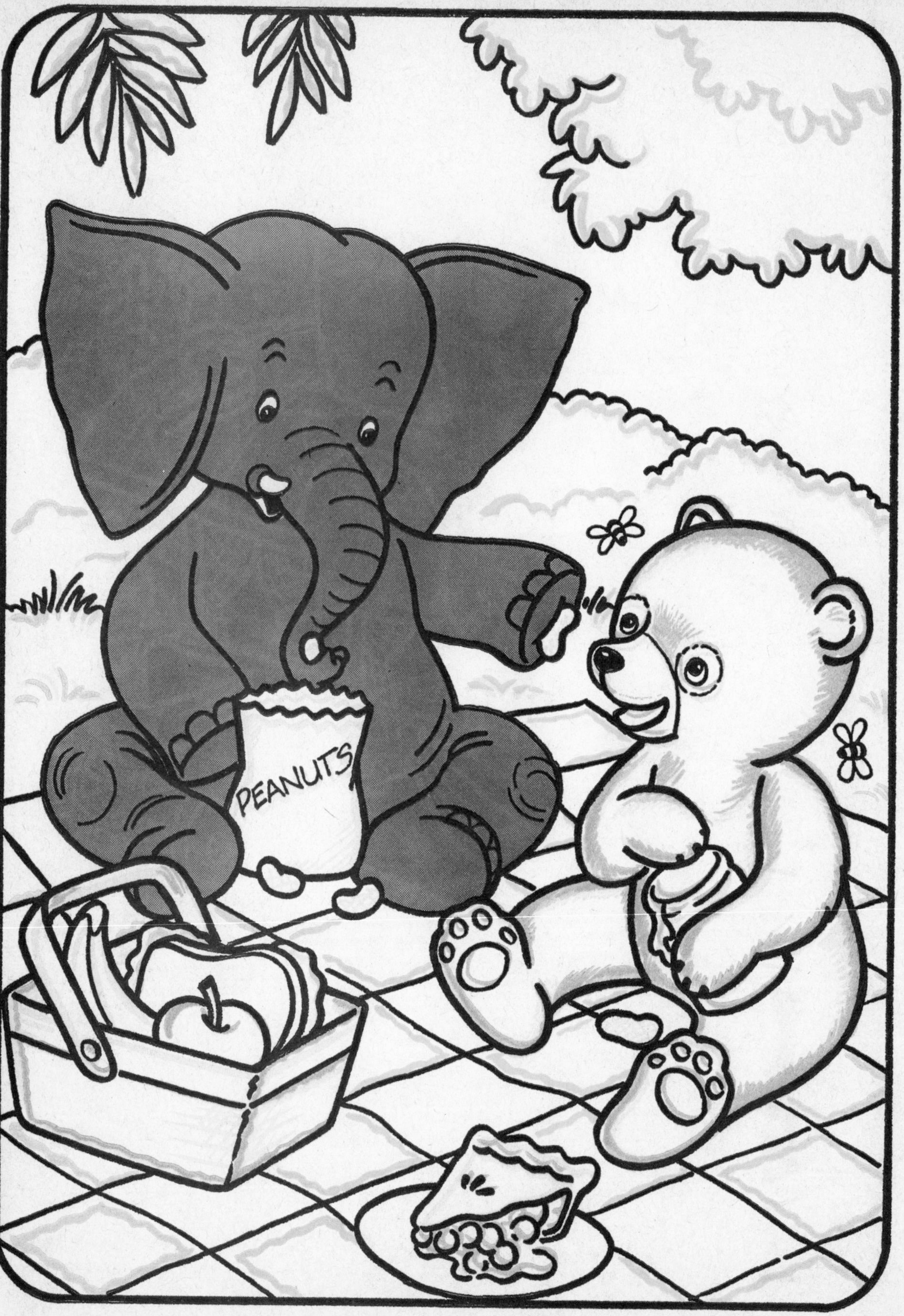
PEANUTS

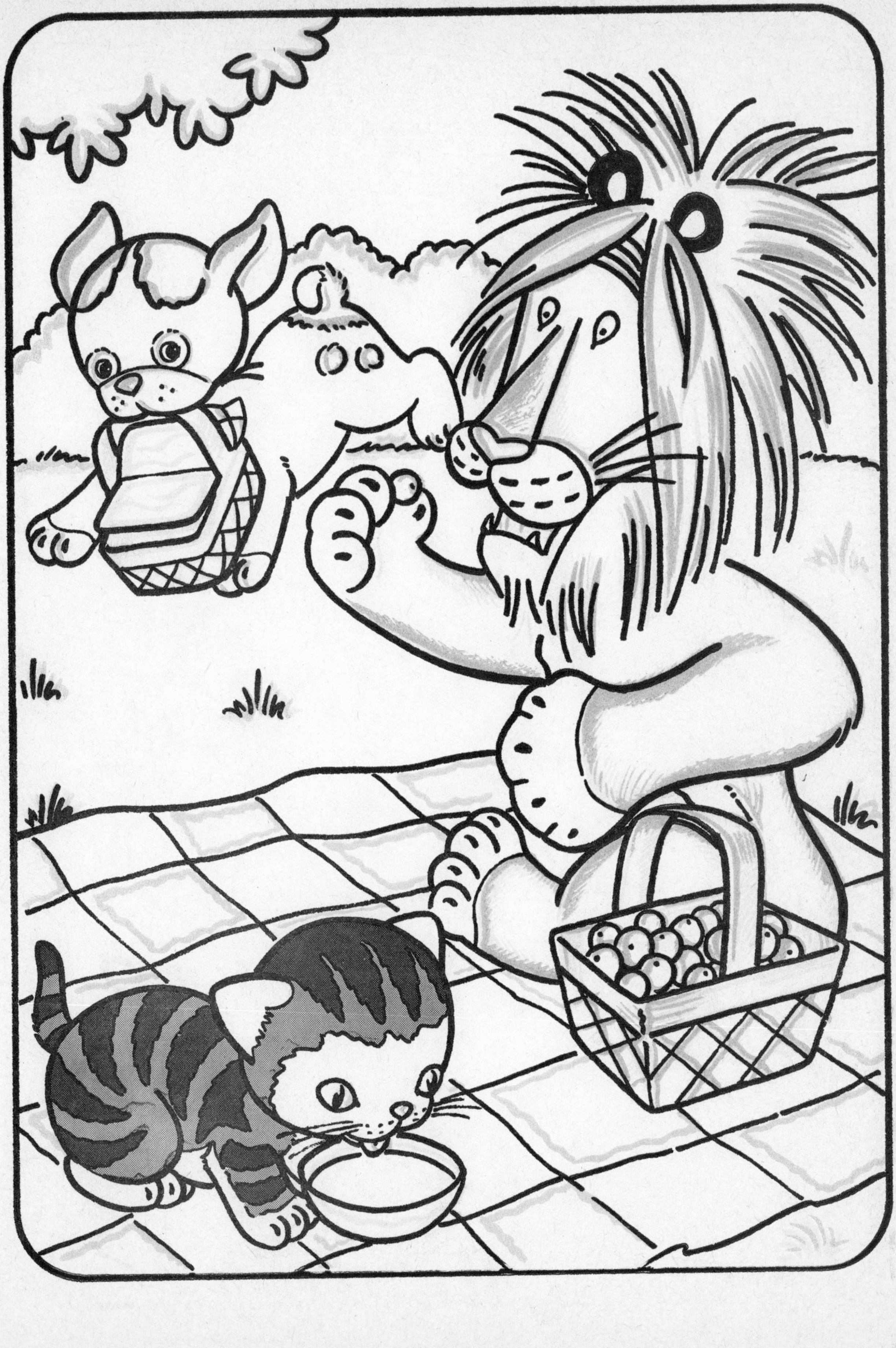

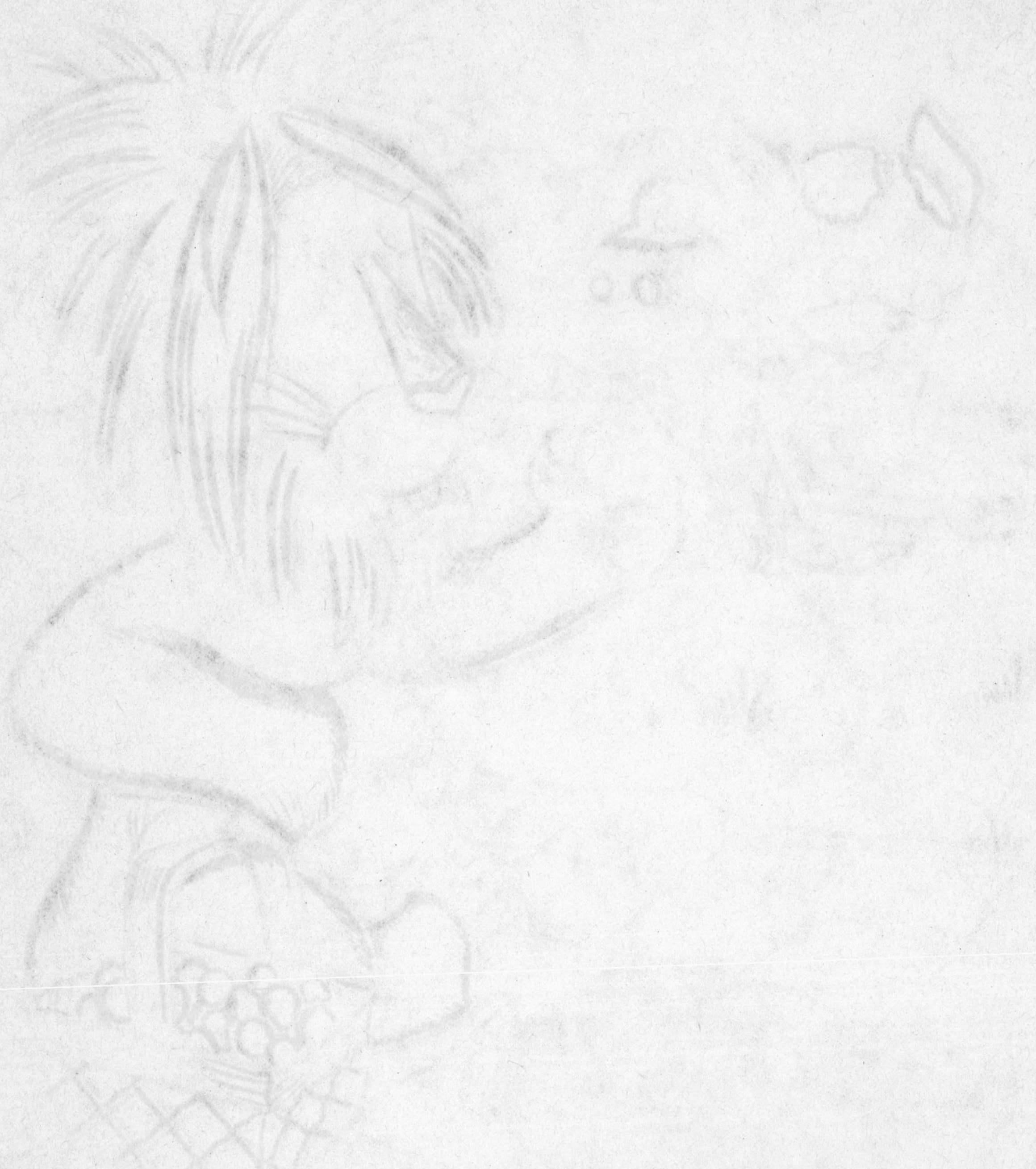

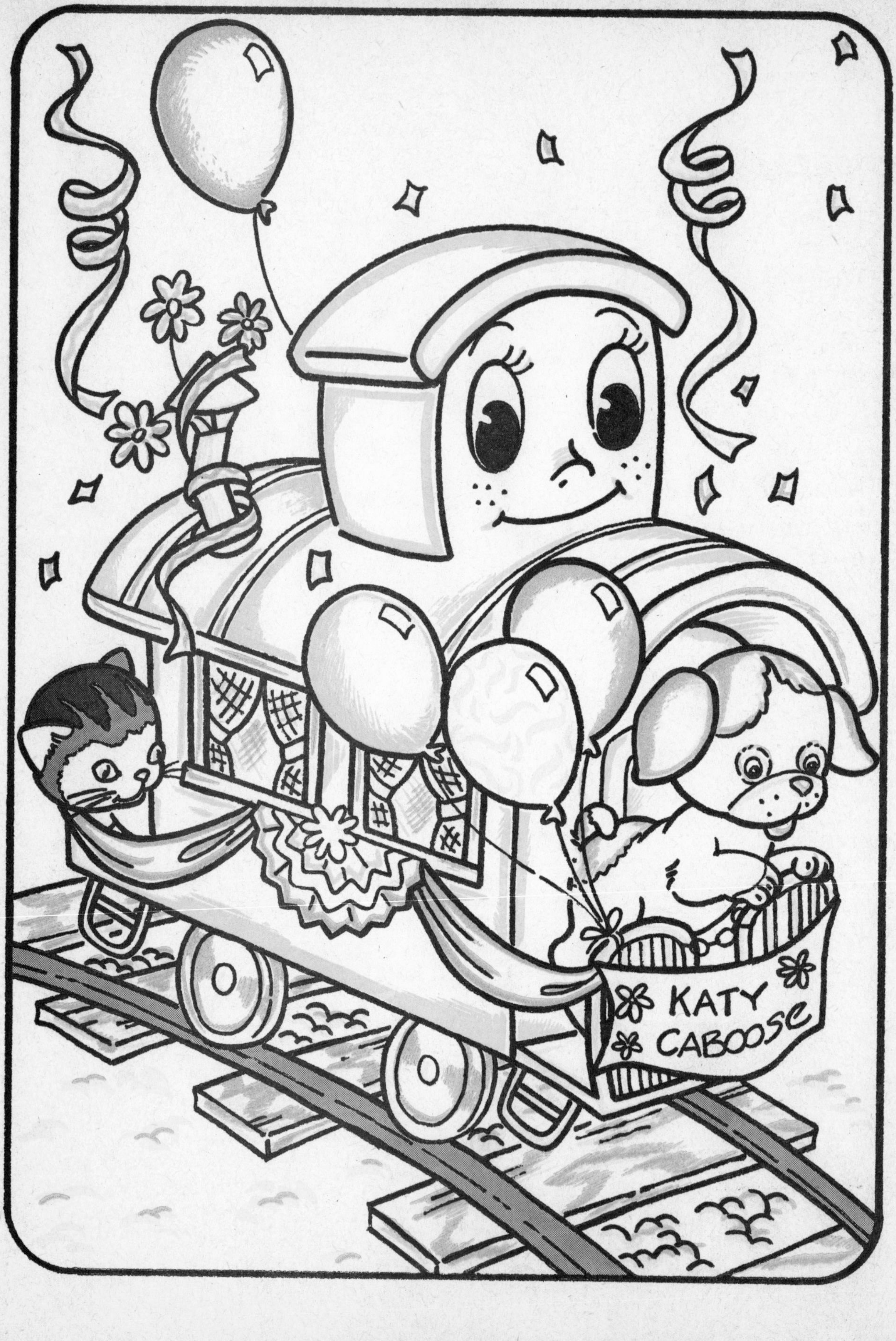
KATY
CABOOSE